Attention,
Girls!

A Guide to Learn All About Your AD/HD

By Patricia O. Quinn, MD

Illustrated by Carl Pearce

Magination Press
Washington, DC
American Psychological Association

This book is dedicated to my beautiful granddaughters—
Caroline, Frannie, Anna, Georgia, and Fiona—with much love, *Nana*

Published by
MAGINATION PRESS
An Educational Publishing Foundation Book
American Psychological Association
750 First Street, NE
Washington, DC 20002

For more information about our books, including a complete catalog, please write to us, call 1-800-374-2721, or visit our website at www.maginationpress.com.

Book design by Naylor Design, Inc., Washington, DC
Printed by Worzalla, Stevens Point, Wisconsin

Library of Congress Cataloging-in-Publication Data

Quinn, Patricia O.
  Attention, girls! : a guide to learn all about your AD/HD / by Patricia O. Quinn ; illustrated by Carl Pearce.
     p. cm.
  ISBN-13: 978-1-4338-0447-2 (hardcover : alk. paper)
  ISBN-10: 1-4338-0447-6 (hardcover : alk. paper)
  ISBN-13: 978-1-4338-0448-9 (pbk. : alk. paper)
  ISBN-10: 1-4338-0448-4 (pbk. : alk. paper) 1. Attention-deficit disorder in adolescence—Juvenile literature. I. Pearce, Carl, ill. II. Title.
  RJ506.H9Q54816 2009
  618.92'8589—dc22
                                    2008054524

10 9 8 7 6

A Note of *Thanks*

As with any book, there are many people I would like to
thank for their help in getting this book into print.

First, to the three young girls with AD/HD (and their
parents) who volunteered to read the first draft and whose
comments were invaluable during the book's infancy.
You know who you are!

Second, to my friends and colleagues, Judith Stern and
Dr. Jeffrey Katz, and to my sister, Kathy Rivenburg. Thanks to
all of you for reading the early manuscript and offering your
expert opinions and words of encouragement.

And last, but not least, to my wonderful editor, Becky
Shaw, whose enthusiasm for the project and helpful tips to
improve the book kept me going and supported my feeling
that I had something wonderful and interesting to offer
young girls.

Table of *Contents*

Read This First!

Hello! My name is Dr. Quinn, and I'm a medical doctor. My specialty is taking care of and working with kids just like you, kids with Attention Deficit Hyperactivity Disorder (AD/HD). I'd like to share some of the things that I have learned about AD/HD, but first let me tell you more about myself and my sister.

When I was seven years old, I liked to play by myself for hours. I would daydream and talk to myself, making up wonderful stories in my head. Often, I wouldn't even hear my mom calling me. I also liked to read, but I would get so interested in a book that I would forget to do other things. I did well in school and liked to study. My mom helped me a lot, especially with my spelling homework. (She was REALLY good in spelling when she was in school.)

I had four sisters (I was the oldest) and we all played together. One of my younger sisters used to get in trouble a lot at school and at home. She was always doing really silly and sometimes even dangerous things. When we were in elementary school, I used to get called into the principal's office to take her home or to tell my mom and dad what she had done. I didn't like that, but I think she liked it even less than I did. I guess she didn't want to be in trouble all the time.

Although I didn't have problems in elementary school like my sister, when I grew up and went to medical school to become a doctor, I noticed that the other students could read and study much faster than I could. I had to read things over and over again because I couldn't remember what I had just read, and rereading took a lot of extra time.

That was when I first began to think that I had problems that others didn't, and I realized I was different in some way.

My sister and I didn't find out we had AD/HD until many years later. You see, until recently AD/HD was thought of as a boys' disorder. Girls just were never diagnosed or weren't diagnosed until they were teens (or even adults), like me and my sister. But now we know that AD/HD occurs in both boys and girls. And we also know how to help girls like you take control of their AD/HD and their lives.

I became a doctor to help kids understand and learn to deal with their personal challenges and school struggles. That's also why I wrote this book. I want to help you learn more about AD/HD so that you can take control of your attention disorder much earlier than my sister and I did. I've learned that understanding and managing AD/HD is not easy, but it is important so that you can do and be your best.

In this book, I hope to answer your questions about AD/HD. In it, you'll meet girls, just like you, who struggle with their AD/HD and its symptoms. You'll learn how to deal with challenges. You'll get tips, strategies, and advice on how to improve the areas of your life affected by AD/HD: schoolwork, friends, feelings, self-esteem, and organization. Most important, I hope this book will help you feel more confident in and better about yourself! By understanding and managing your AD/HD, you'll be able to focus, not on how your attention disorder affects your life, but on doing what you do best—being a kid!

Before you start reading this book, let's talk about how you might want to use it. First of all, you don't have to read it from cover to cover. You can jump around or go straight to the information you want and need. For example, if you've just been diagnosed with AD/HD and you're still learning what it is (or if you just want some more background information), you should probably start at Part 1. But if you want to learn about how to make and keep friends, you can go straight to Chapter 9. Or if you're struggling to get organized at school and at home and you want to tackle those problems right away, Chapter 4 is the section for you.

Come back to *Attention, Girls!* whenever you need to check out more information or when new problems arise. Remember that this book is just the beginning. You have lots of support out there. Your parents, teachers, friends, siblings, and coaches are all here to help. In other words, you don't have to do this alone! As you're reading this book (or after you've finished it), you may want to show or loan it to your parents, counselor, or friends so they can better understand what you're going through and how they can best support you. Armed with the information from this book and with the support of your family, friends, and other important people in your life, you'll be on your way to successfully managing your AD/HD and feeling great about yourself.

Another "girl" with AD/HD,

Patricia O. Quinn, MD

Part One

Get the 411 on AD/HD!

Chapter One
What Is AD/HD Anyway?

Maddie was confused. She didn't see why her teacher had asked her parents to come to school for a meeting with the school counselor. Yes, she sometimes forgot her homework, and she did daydream in class, but did that mean she had AD/HD? She certainly wasn't always getting into trouble and bothering other kids like Michael who had AD/HD. Could she have AD/HD? And what did that mean? Was there something wrong with her or her brain? Yikes!

If you are like Maddie and someone has told you that you have AD/HD, I'll bet you have lots of questions, too. But before I answer those questions, let's spend a few minutes talking about what AD/HD is and what it is not.

What Is AD/HD?

AD/HD or Attention Deficit Hyperactivity Disorder is a real disorder that is thought to be present from birth. It is best understood as a set of behaviors that lead to difficulty paying attention and focusing. These behaviors can include distractibility, impulsivity, hyperactivity, disorganization, carelessness, and poor time management. (I'll talk about these behaviors later in this chapter.) Having AD/HD can definitely make it harder for you to control yourself and pay attention. School may be difficult, or you may feel that you're always in trouble. AD/HD affects each person differently, so you might not have the same set of behaviors as another kid with AD/HD. And that can be very confusing for you as well as your parents and other adults.

What Causes AD/HD?

AD/HD is a medical condition. It is seen in kids when certain areas of their brains are not working the way they should. To understand AD/HD better, let's take a look at how the brain works and what scientists think goes wrong when someone has AD/HD.

Your brain works a lot like a computer network. It's the control center for your thinking, learning, actions, and behaviors. It keeps your life on track and stores lots of information. Your brain is made up of cells called neurons. These cells work like mini-computers wired together in your brain, but they don't actually touch.

Attention, Attention!

Your brain has several layers that play a role in controlling both your attention and activity levels.

- The **cortex** is for thinking, learning, problem-solving, and planning ahead.

- The **subcortex** controls your emotions and contains the reward center that allows us to enjoy things that you like. It also connects the outer cortex to the lower levels or brain stem.

- The **brain stem** is where automatic functions like breathing and digestion are controlled.

They're separated by tiny spaces called synapses. Neurons communicate with each other by sending messages across synapses using chemicals (neurotransmitters). This process is kind of like when you send an e-mail to your friend from your computer. In order to send that e-mail (message) from your computer (neuron) to another computer (neuron), it has to travel across cyberspace (synapse) using the Internet (neurotransmitter). Scientists think that AD/HD is caused when there are problems with these neurotransmitters. If the Internet is down, e-mail won't go through!

Now, many kids with AD/HD worry when they hear that there is something wrong with their brain. (That's understandable!) Trouble with getting messages to the right areas explain what is going on in your brain and why you have problems paying attention, getting organized, or remembering things. But these areas are not damaged! There are lots of ways that will get them working again. Better yet, these areas have nothing to do with how smart, talented, or athletic you are. Kids with AD/HD are as smart, funny, and creative as other kids!

What Behaviors Do Kids With AD/HD Have?

The following behaviors are often seen in kids with AD/HD and are usually the reasons they have problems or get into trouble:

Inattentiveness

Distractibility

Carelessness

Disorganization

Hyperactivity

Impulsivity

Kids with AD/HD are as smart, funny, and creative as other kids!

Let's talk about each of these behaviors a little more.

INATTENTIVENESS

Inattentiveness is difficulty focusing on one thing or having a short attention span. This makes it difficult to concentrate and stay focused. Because you are not paying attention, you have problems following directions or you might forget what you are supposed to be doing.

Sometimes it's difficult for adults to understand that kids with AD/HD have problems paying attention because kids with AD/HD *can* pay attention, sometimes for a very long time, especially when they are interested in an activity. For example, you may be able to watch TV, play computer games, or read your favorite book for hours, but you can't seem to concentrate and stay focused to read three chapters of a book assigned for homework or to complete 60 math problems. It may be hard for you to sit and concentrate on your work in class, complete a puzzle, or play a board game for very long, but you could play outdoors or at the pool forever.

DISTRACTIBILITY

Distractibility means that your attention is easily drawn away from what you are doing. If you have AD/HD, you may be easily distracted by other things going on around you or by noises in or outside the room you are in. Because of the problem you have concentrating on just one thing, it becomes hard for you to stay on track and get your work done. You may find that you are always switching what you are doing and that you don't finish many of the projects that you start.

Kids with AD/HD also find that they are not only distracted by things going on around them, but that they can be distracted by thoughts going on inside their own heads. We call this daydreaming. If you find yourself frequently thinking about other things or going on adventures in your head, you're probably a daydreamer. Daydreaming

Sara's Daydreaming Problems

Daydreaming always gets me into trouble! I know I'm daydreaming at school when . . .

- I think about the toys in my bedroom and imagine that I'm playing with them instead of paying attention to the lesson.

- I get confused about where I am because I daydream I'm somewhere else.

- I sometimes don't hear someone calling my name. When I finally do, I look up and all of the girls are staring at me. They start laughing and I get really embarrassed.

may be fun and may be more interesting than what your teacher is talking about, but it can also cause problems for you. When you stop daydreaming, you may feel lost or confused. Because you missed the directions for an assignment you might not know what to do next or when the assignment is due. If you miss part of a conversation going on around you, you might not be sure of what your friends are talking about and you won't know what to say. You can miss out on a lot of important information if you daydream too much or are very distracted.

CARELESSNESS

Carelessness refers to making mistakes and forgetting things. When you don't pay careful attention, begin your work without reading or waiting for the directions, or work too quickly, you can make mistakes on your homework and tests. How many times has your teacher asked you if you've read the directions? Do you have problems finding your clothes, jackets, shoes, or toys because you can't remember where you put them? If you are careless, you may frequently lose or misplace your belongings or important papers, like your homework, a signed permission slip, or a note for your parents from your teacher.

DISORGANIZATION

Disorganization means having trouble getting and staying organized. It can cause you to have problems keeping track of your things or your time. You can imagine how all of these problems with paying attention to details and following directions can cause someone with AD/HD to look disorganized. And chances are you probably *are* disorganized if you often look that way! Your room, desk, or backpack may be messy, making it more difficult for you to find your things.

If you are disorganized, you may also not be very good at making decisions, choosing what you want to or should do next, or managing your time. You may find yourself starting and stopping projects or games as you change your mind or get bored. A project with too may steps that need to be done in a certain order may cause you to lose track of what you are supposed to be doing next. When you have several things to do at once, prioritizing what to do first to get started can also be difficult. Some kids with AD/HD say they have so many ideas that it is hard for them to choose just one to work on. You may also lose track of time or misjudge how long it will take you to complete a project. If you are disorganized, you may always be late or rushing to get something done.

HYPERACTIVITY

Hyperactivity is defined as excessive body movements that are usually without a purpose and greater than normally seen at a certain age. Basically, it's when you move around a lot. If you are hyperactive, you might have difficulty sitting still or staying in one place for very long. You may feel restless, have lots of energy, and prefer to be "on the go" or playing, running, and jumping. When you are asked to stop moving, you might be able to do it for a little while, but it's really hard for you.

Hyperactivity does not look the same in everyone. Instead of running around, you may be fidgety and feel you need to move your hands and feet a lot. You may twirl your hair, play with a small toy, or doodle with your pencil. Doodling on papers or books is common for kids with AD/HD. Sometimes doodling helps them to stay focused and to listen better, but sometimes it keeps them from paying attention. Remember that even though the word "hyperactivity" is in the name AD/HD, not all kids with AD/HD are hyperactive.

IMPULSIVITY

Impulsivity is doing or saying something without thinking about it first. If you have AD/HD, you may be impulsive and act or say things without thinking of the consequences. For example, you know that you are not supposed to ride your bike in the park without telling your mom or dad where you are going. But if you really want to get to the playground on the other side, you may forget the rule and ride in the park anyway. Acting impulsively can get you into trouble and cause you to do things that you regret afterwards, like saying something to a friend that you wish you hadn't or leaving your field trip group at the zoo to look at the lion cubs.

Acting impulsively can get you into trouble.

Are There Different Kinds of AD/HD?

There is only one AD/HD, but experts have divided AD/HD into three types depending on the behaviors seen together most often. The three types are called:

Inattentive-distractible type
Hyperactive-impulsive type
Combined type

Combined type is the most common type. Kids with this type of AD/HD usually have all of the behaviors seen in AD/HD that we've talked about above. In general, girls most often have the inattentive-distractible type of AD/HD where problems with attention and distractibility are the most common complaints. The hyperactive-impulsive type is the least common of all of the types of AD/HD in both boys and girls and occurs only in about 3% of boys and 1% of girls with AD/HD.

Do Many Kids Have AD/HD?

About 1 in every 10 kids has some kind of trouble paying attention, but not all of them have AD/HD. Some kids have trouble paying attention because they're sad or have problems at home with their families or because they don't get enough sleep. About 4.8 million children are thought to have AD/HD in the United States, and about 2 million of them have already been diagnosed. AD/HD is not just seen in the United States. It can be found in every country around the world. Kids in places like Germany, Sweden, China, South Africa, Australia, Brazil, and Japan also have AD/HD. When you think about it that means that many millions of kids all over the world have AD/HD! It's not really rare and if you have AD/HD, you are definitely not alone!

You are definitely not alone!

Is There Any Good Stuff About AD/HD?

At times, you may feel people are often frustrated or upset with you, that your life is out of your control, and that things are not going very well, but having AD/HD is not all bad. There are some good things about having AD/HD. Can you think of any? I can!

Your high energy levels will usually allow you to use your muscles and get lots of exercise. You probably can run and play for hours. You might be very creative and talented at crafts or drawing. Maybe you are good at discovering new ways to have fun or thinking up games for you and your friends to play. You may be able to look at things a little differently and come up with several really good and unique approaches to solving puzzles or problems. You might also have a great sense of humor and find it easy to make other people laugh. Everyone is unique and we all have strengths as well as

Attention, Attention!

Sometimes your AD/HD (and all that it brings with it) can give you a boost. You could think about using all that energy to excel in sports. Do you remember Michael Phelps winning those medals in the Olympics? Well, he has AD/HD and had trouble in school and with friends when he was your age. I've also known girls with AD/HD who have become scientists, writers, actresses, and fashion designers.

weaknesses. Take time to think about some of the good things in your life that may have come to you because you have AD/HD.

So, How Do You Get AD/HD?

You can't catch AD/HD. In most cases, AD/HD is something that you were born with. It's just part of who you are like your brown eyes, your curly hair, or your cat allergies. AD/HD in most cases is inherited (usually occurs in the same family), so you may have a brother, cousin, mother, father, uncle, or aunt with AD/HD, too. In fact, if a parent has AD/HD, there is a very good chance that their child will have AD/HD.

Attention, Attention!

My AD/HD has helped me in many ways—most important, I learned not to give up. My AD/HD made some things difficult, but I knew that if I kept trying and asked for help when I needed it, I'd eventually accomplish what I started out to do. I have lots of great ideas and the energy to get most of them done. As a result, I have been able to write several books for kids and adults with AD/HD and have helped people better understand AD/HD.

This chapter has contained a lot of (boring) facts, but I hope it has helped you understand what AD/HD is and what causes it. One of the important first steps in dealing with any problem is finding out as much about it as you can, and that is what I have tried to do here. Now that we know a lot about AD/HD, we can take action and help you better manage your behaviors and deal with your feelings. But before we do that, let's take a closer look at the many different ways AD/HD can present in kids as we meet some other girls with AD/HD in the next chapter.

Chapter Two

How Does AD/HD Make Me Act?

Maddie read some books about AD/HD that her mom bought for her and she looked up AD/HD on the Internet, but all of these books were about boys. She had learned a lot about AD/HD, but she still wondered, "How do girls with AD/HD act and feel?"

In the last chapter, I talked about the behaviors we see when someone has AD/HD and the three types of AD/HD based on those behaviors. In this chapter, I will introduce you and Maddie to several girls with AD/HD. Each of these girls has one of the types of AD/HD I described earlier. The kids you'll meet soon include:

Girls with hyperactive-impulsive type
Girls with inattentive-distractible type
Girls with combined type

Their stories are all different, but each one has AD/HD. Maybe you will read about someone that has the same problems or acts like you in these stories. It is important to remember that the behaviors seen with AD/HD appear different in different girls and that some of

the behaviors in these stories might overlap. So, don't be surprised if you find that you act like more than one of the girls described here.

Girls With Hyperactive-Impulsive Type

As you'll recall, hyperactivity means moving around a lot, and impulsivity is saying or doing something without thinking about it first. So, hyperactive-impulsive type of AD/HD includes kids who have more difficulty with keeping still when they need to and who frequently act before they think things through. Let's take a look at three girls who definitely have these problems.

HYPERACTIVE HANNAH

Hannah has such problems sitting still. When she watches TV, she lies all over the sofa or floor and usually has her feet on the wall or furniture. She never just sits in a chair or on the sofa. When her family has dinner, she doesn't stay in her seat very long either. She wolfs down her food and can't wait to do something else more exciting. She asks to be excused before the rest of her family is finished or hops up to answer the phone or to get something from the fridge. Her mother often asks her if there is a tack on her chair and teases her that maybe that is the reason why she can't stay in her chair. This has become a family joke. When the family takes a long car trip, Hanna's brothers and sister don't want to sit next to her because she is always moving around in her seat, kicking her feet, and bothering them.

Teachers have noticed Hannah's problem in school as well. Hannah often leans over her desk or sits on the top of her chair. Other kids say she is bothering them and her teacher is afraid she will fall. When Hannah feels restless, she asks to leave the room or gets up to look out the window or sharpen her pencil. When all of the other kids in class are quietly listening to the teacher, you can be sure that Hannah will cause some kind of noise.

FIDGETY FIONA

Fiona is not hyperactive like Hannah, but she still has trouble being still. Fiona doesn't get out of her chair, but she squirms, wiggles, and jiggles her legs. She also twirls her hair or plays with her barrettes or hair scrunchies. Because she needs to keep busy, Fiona will often line up her collection of little erasers on her desk or rearrange her pencil box when she should be paying attention to the teacher.

Fiona also does other things that bother people. Sometimes she hums or sings to herself. When people ask her to stop, she doesn't know what they are talking about because she didn't even know she was humming. When Fiona chews gum, she thinks it's fun to stretch it out of her mouth to see how far it will go. This is annoying, especially when it gets stuck on her face or tangled in her hair. Her mom is always telling her to keep her gum in her mouth.

At the dinner table, Fiona gets into trouble for tapping her foot on the rung of her chair, lining up her vegetables, or making designs with the food on her plate. Fiona feels badly because she doesn't mean for her behaviors to upset other people.

CRYBABY CHRISTINE

Christine is eight years old and she finds herself crying or getting frustrated easily. She gets embarrassed because she can't keep from crying. It seems that everything makes her cry. If her team is losing, she cries. If her mother says "no" to her when she asks for something, she cries. If her friends are talking about someone and she can't hear them clearly, she thinks they are talking about her and she cries. Her parents get angry with her when she cries, and her friends are starting to make fun of her. People just don't seem to realize that she doesn't want to cry all the time. She wants things to change, but she doesn't know how to stop it.

Christine also has a temper and can throw tantrums when she gets frustrated or upset. She gets angry, throws things, stomps her feet, or cries and screams if anyone says "no" to her or if she has to wait for something she wants right away. She doesn't want to act like this but she can't seem to stop and think or use her words to describe how she is feeling. No matter how hard she tries to stay calm, she usually just reacts. Christine could be described as hyper-reactive and impulsive rather than hyperactive.

Girls With Inattentive-Distractible Type

Inattentiveness, as we talked about in the last chapter, is having a short attention span, and distractibility is having trouble staying focused on just one thing. Girls who are inattentive and easily distracted have this type of AD/HD. Let's meet some of those girls now.

SHY SAMANTHA

Samantha likes to sit in the back of the class. She used to try to answer questions in class, but after being embarrassed because she answered some questions incorrectly, Samantha doesn't raise her hand to answer a question any more, even if she knows the correct answer. Teachers tell her parents that she doesn't participate in class discussions, even when they encourage her to speak up. Samantha is happiest if no one notices her and is upset if they do. She can get really nervous when she's in a new place or if there are a lot of people around, like at a big birthday party for a friend. Samantha gives up pretty quickly if she can't do something right the first time or if work is difficult for her. Because it takes her longer to understand what she has to do, some people think Samantha is not interested or just not as smart as the other kids. Samantha never gets into trouble and might even be considered "slow" or "lazy" by some people, even though she really is not. No one would ever say that she was hyperactive.

Samantha's shyness causes problems when it comes to making friends. She is so shy she doesn't feel good, and it's hard for her to join groups where she doesn't know the other kids. She ends up so worried about what others may think that she can't say or do anything. Samantha has one good friend, Cathi that she has played with since she was a little girl. But Cathi has moved recently and doesn't live near enough to visit. Now they don't see each other very often and Samantha feels lonely.

SPACEY SARA

Sara likes to daydream. She likes to visit far away places in her head and dreams of having adventures with her favorite friends when she should be paying attention in class instead. When Sara comes back from daydreaming, she finds that she hasn't heard what the teacher was saying. Once, she even missed the school bus to go home because she was daydreaming when her bus number was called.

Sara has discovered that she can focus on things that she likes and can play for hours when she gets really involved. This is not the case when something is boring to her like homework or cleaning her room. When Sara is playing with her jewelry-making kits, she's so interested that she doesn't even hear when her mother calls her for dinner. That makes her mom pretty mad. Her mother really doesn't understand how Sara can make bracelets and necklaces for hours but can't pay attention enough to get her homework done.

Because Sara doesn't pay attention and because she is so often lost in her own daydreams, Sara's mom says she doesn't feel that Sara lives on the same planet. She will sometimes call out, "Earth to Sara!" Sara's mother doesn't think that Sara could have AD/HD since she is so spacey and dreamy and not the least bit active.

DISORGANIZED DORA

Dora has decided she is just plain messy. She can't keep anything straight. Her room is a mess with her clothes all over the floor and hanging out of the drawers. She can't find anything and her games often have missing pieces when she wants to play with them. She tries to turn in neat papers in class, but they usually end up with lots of erasing, and once she even had a hole in an assignment from erasing too much.

Dora is tired of losing everything, but she really doesn't know what to do about it. Her problems with not being organized also keep her from turning her assignments and projects in on time. When she got a "D" on a project because she turned it in a week late, she promised herself and her parents that it would not happen again. But, here it is the night before her project for science class on the solar system is due, and she doesn't have any of the supplies that she needs. Looks like she'll be late, again! This makes Dora feel frustrated and disappointed in herself. Sometimes she feels she can't do anything right no matter how hard she tries.

ANXIOUS ANNA

Anna worries a lot about school and her friends. Because she has trouble paying attention, she worries that she'll forget to do something important. She worries that she might have a test that she's forgotten about or that she's left an important book at home, so she checks and rechecks her backpack. All this worrying has caused her to have lots of stomachaches.

Anna thinks that the other girls don't like her. When she sees two girls talking together, she worries that they are talking about her. Sometimes her worrying prevents her from falling asleep at night. She just lies in bed and thinks about things that might go wrong. Anna is tired of worrying, but she doesn't know what to do about it. Her parents are worried about her. It seems everyone in her family is worried!

FORGETFUL FRANNIE

Frannie's dad often teases her that he's afraid that she will forget her own name, because Frannie is always forgetting things. She has lost three jackets and her very best tennis racket because she couldn't remember where she put them. This situation would be bad enough, but Frannie also forgets what other people tell her. She forgets when the teacher tells the class what the homework is or when they will have a test. She also forgets to bring home notes or to get permission slips signed. That is why she missed the last class trip to the aquarium. The rest of the class got to go, but she had to stay with the kids in the next class when she forgot to return her signed slip. She even forgot to go to her friend's birthday party. That was very embarrassing and made her feel very badly about herself! How is she ever going to get over this forgetfulness? Maybe her dad is right and she'll eventually even forget her name.

Girls With Combined Type

Combined type is the most common type of AD/HD. Kids with this type usually have all of the behaviors seen in AD/HD that we've already discussed. Let's meet a few of these girls to get a picture of what having this type looks like.

CHATTY CAROLINE

Caroline just seems to talk all the time. In school it is really difficult for her to be quiet and to pay attention to her own work. Caroline's last report card warned, "She's talking entirely too much while group work is in progress. She needs to find a more productive use of her time rather than interfering with other students after she has completed her assignments."

Caroline tends to say whatever comes into her head and sometimes that gets her into trouble. It has also hurt other people's feelings and she really doesn't mean to do that. Caroline's friends complain that she interrupts them, butts in, and is too bossy. Her mother and father sometimes ask her to be quiet and stop talking for just a little while, but even that is hard for her to do.

TOMBOY TATIANA

Tatiana is 10 years old and loves to be outside and moving around rather than sitting in school. She likes summer and vacations the best! Tatiana plays soccer, basketball, and likes to go fishing with her dad.

Tatiana has always been very active and likes excitement. She learned to ride a two-wheeled bike without training wheels the week before her fourth birthday. When she was in kindergarten, recess was her favorite time. She loved to climb up to the top of the jungle gym on the playground or play in the sandbox for hours if she could. She still doesn't mind getting dirty or having skinned knees.

Thomas has been Tatiana's best friend since preschool. She says that they like to do a lot of the same things and that she would rather play with boys because she thinks girls are boring and talk too much.

In school, Tatiana's written work is messy and her teacher often writes, "Messy, do over! You can do better, Tatiana!" on her papers and has sent notes home to her parents. The last note said, "Tatiana continues to have problems sitting still and doing her written work. She rushes through her math problems and makes many careless mistakes. All her papers are usually very messy. She would do better spending her energy taking her time and checking her work, rather than doodling on her papers!" These notes and comments by the teacher are starting to bother Tatiana and she's beginning to not want to go to school anymore.

GRUMPY GEORGIA

Georgia is hyper-sensitive rather than hyperactive. She finds that lots of things bother her and that makes her grumpy and irritable. Clothes are a good example. She really feels more comfortable in loose, soft clothes that aren't too tight in the waist. Tags in her shirts scratch and make her skin itchy. She has to ask her mom to cut them out. Georgia doesn't like to get her hair washed or brushed and she just began taking showers in third grade. Noises also bother her. It seems she can hear sounds like fans or airplanes before other people notice them and, if it is too noisy, it hurts her ears. Her mom says that Georgia is just too sensitive, but what can she do? Often it is hard for her to concentrate when so many things are distracting her and making her feel all irritable and prickly.

After meeting all of these girls, you can see that they are all very different, yet they all have AD/HD. When a girl has AD/HD, she may not look or act exactly like any one of these girls, but rather be a combination of several of them. Do you have any of these problems? Are you shy like Samantha or worried like Anna? Do you have problems sitting still like Hannah or do you daydream like Sara?

Boys With AD/HD

Chances are you know at least one boy with AD/HD—your brother or cousin, your neighbor or best friend. If this is the case, you've probably gotten to learn about their problems caused by AD/HD or at least see how they behave. You also might have heard people on the news, in school, or even at home talk about boys with AD/HD. That's because a lot of people associate AD/HD only with boys and their behaviors. Boys with AD/HD are generally disruptive and aggressive. They tend to be hyperactive and can get into more fights than other boys.

For many years, it was thought that more boys had AD/HD than girls did. For every 10 boys with AD/HD, only *one* girl was found. And it was thought that if girls didn't act exactly like the boys with AD/HD, they didn't have AD/HD. This is simply not true! AD/HD in girls just seems different. Girls may behave very differently from boys with AD/HD in many ways, but their (and your) AD/HD is no less severe. Compared to girls with AD/HD, boys are:

More disruptive
More hyperactive and aggressive
Less inattentive and disorganized

Let's talk about each of these so you can see how AD/HD in boys and girls can seem different. This should help you better understand your AD/HD and explain it to people who might not know why you might behave differently from boys with the disorder.

MORE DISRUPTIVE

Boys with AD/HD tend to be more disruptive than girls. In school, boys with AD/HD might interrupt the teacher while he's giving a lesson, or break up a group of kids playing during recess. They might be class clowns and draw lots of attention to themselves. These boys also tend to get into trouble a lot, both at home and at school, because of their disruptive behavior, like talking out of turn, making a lot of unnecessary noise, or bothering other kids. Unlike boys, girls with AD/HD typically do not call attention to themselves. They tend to not get into trouble and are not usually disruptive in school. They may even be shy and sit in the back of the class like

Samantha. That is one reason why their AD/HD is often missed until they are in middle or high school, when they have more problems with schoolwork.

MORE HYPERACTIVE AND AGGRESSIVE

Boys, in general, are more hyperactive than girls. Girls can have AD/HD with hyperactivity, but their hyperactive behaviors often seem different than boys'. Instead of running around, a girl who is hyperactive might have trouble sitting still in her chair. In the classroom, she might sit on the desk behind her chair or lean over the girl in front. She will wiggle, move around a lot, and bother others, but she is often unaware that she's doing this. When excited, she might call out an answer in class without raising her hand or throw her backpack in the air because she is happy that she doesn't have any homework.

A girl with AD/HD can also be hyper-talkative rather than hyper-active. She may talk a lot or frequently butt into others' conversations like Caroline. These girls tend to just say whatever comes into their heads and that often causes them to hurt other people's feelings or get into trouble.

Boys with AD/HD can sometimes get into physical fights. Girls with AD/HD do not usually get into physical fights, but they can be verbally aggressive, using words to hurt others. They may also have problems getting along with other girls, if they are too bossy or impulsively say whatever comes into their heads, like Caroline does. These behaviors can turn off the other girls. As a result, girls with AD/HD may feel that no one likes them or that they do not have many friends.

In general, girls with AD/HD are more likely to have problems controlling their emotions than their actions, making them hyper-reactive rather than hyperactive. They might cry, have tantrums, or slam doors like Christine. Christine is usually able to sit and quietly do her homework at the dining room table without needing to get up and move around, but just last week, Christine ran to her room and slammed the door when she became frustrated while she was doing her math homework.

A girl who is hyper-reactive might yell at someone on the bus because that other girl sat in her seat. She might also have trouble controlling her temper during basketball games, and she might cry easily, particularly if her team is losing. She always feels sorry and embarrassed about her behaviors afterwards, but can't seem to control herself at the time. When she is excited she might not be able to calm down and then get into trouble for being too rough or too loud or carrying on for too long.

LESS INATTENTIVE AND DISORGANIZED

Compared to boys, girls with AD/HD tend to have more problems with attention than with hyperactivity. This trouble concentrating often affects schoolwork, but some girls with AD/HD work very hard and put in a lot of effort, and despite their AD/HD, they can do very well in school for many years. Even so, these girls may need more help keeping organized and on track. Like Dora, they often feel frustrated. School feels hard for them because of all the problems they need to overcome and the amount of time they need to put in to get good grades. Although they can do the work, it takes them a long time to get through it, and as a result, these girls with AD/HD often say that they don't feel very smart or that they feel different from everybody else.

So what you need to realize is that having AD/HD doesn't need to limit who you are in any way. You are just as smart, creative, and funny as anyone else (or maybe even more!). We each have our special gifts, talents, and personalities that make us who we are. Having AD/HD is only one small part of who you are. This book is meant to help you understand and manage this one, little part of you so that you can shine.

Chapter Three

Who Can I Go to for Help?

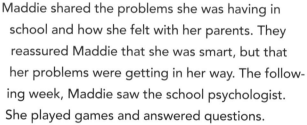

Maddie shared the problems she was having in school and how she felt with her parents. They reassured Maddie that she was smart, but that her problems were getting in her way. The following week, Maddie saw the school psychologist. She played games and answered questions. Maddie also visited her doctor, Dr. Shaw. He examined and talked to Maddie and had her parents and teacher complete forms rating her behaviors. After these tests, the specialists decided that Maddie had AD/HD. They told her and her parents and proposed a plan to help.

By now, you've probably been diagnosed with AD/HD, so you know that it's one of the main things that's been causing the problems that you have at home and at school. If you haven't been diagnosed officially, here's a look at the process and the people involved. First, you and your parents will talk about the problems you've been having at home and school. Your teachers or school counselor might have talked to your parents about your school performance or behaviors, too. Then, your parents may arrange for you to take some tests. You may visit experts such as a counselor or psychologist for paper-and-pencil testing like Maddie. These tests are used to find out how you learn best. They look at how you concentrate, organize information, and focus. They also help to explain your strengths and weaknesses when it comes to schoolwork—what you do well in and what you have problems with.

After gathering all of this information, the experts you've seen will be able to decide if you do have AD/HD and may determine what type. They'll talk with your mom and dad about the results of these paper-and-pencil tests and suggest ways to help you. Sometimes they'll write a report for you and your parents to review. Your parents can also give this report to your teachers and your doctor. You'll also create a plan with these experts and your parents that will help with your AD/HD. If you have questions, ask your parents if you can speak to these experts with them.

Just like getting the diagnosis, managing your AD/HD involves many people, but you are the most important part of the team to make things better in your life. After all, you know yourself better than anybody! But how do you get started? Who will be part of your team? Like Maddie, your team will probably be composed of people who were involved in your diagnosis, adults you see every

You are the most important part of the team.

You know yourself better than anybody!

day, and new people who can really help you excel. These big supporters include:

Your parents
Your teachers
Your school counselor
Your doctor
Your therapist
Your tutor
Your coach

Let's take a look at these important people and how they can help you manage your AD/HD.

Maddie's Plan!

My parents and I set up this plan so that I can manage my AD/HD:

- Work with a tutor once a week.

- Take my medication every day.

- Have my teacher mail my long-term assignment sheets home in envelopes Mom brought in at the beginning of the school year.

- Study with Sasha, my homework buddy.

- Read more books abut AD/HD.

- Set up a schedule at home, to remind me to do my chores and my homework.

Talking to Your Parents

Your parents can be a huge help for you. After all, they just want you to be happy and to do your best! If you're having problems like Maddie, the first thing to do is to talk with your parents about the things that are bothering you. It is important that they understand what is going on in your life at home, in school, and with friends, and how you feel about all of it.

One helpful thing you can do before talking to your parents (or you can do this with them) is to make a list. Write down things that you think are problems for you on that list. We will call these areas your "weaknesses." Now make another list. On this list write down good things about yourself or what you think you do well. These are called "strengths." Everybody has strengths as well as weaknesses. It is important to focus on your strengths and not just on your weaknesses. Sometimes you can even use your strengths to balance out your weaknesses. Your parents can help you identify these qualities, and you can work together to harness your strengths and work with your weaknesses.

Sometimes you can even use your strengths to balance out your weaknesses.

Working With Your Teachers

If you are experiencing problems in class or during the school day, it's important to let your teachers know so that you can get help. Remember, your teachers cannot help you with a problem if they don't know about it! Ask your teacher if there is a time that the two of you can talk when the other kids aren't around. At that meeting, you can privately discuss what has been going on in school including your behaviors, your grades, or your homework assignments. Together you can come up with ways to deal with the problems you are having. Teachers have worked with hundreds of kids and have

Maddie's Talking Tips

Here are some ideas for when you talk to your parents. They helped me!

- Tell them how you feel about having AD/HD. "I feel confused."

- Let them know about your other feelings. "AD/HD makes me sad. I'm always in trouble and I don't feel as smart as the other kids at school."

- Tell them about what you're good at and what's hard for you. "I'm great at art but I have a hard time with math."

Your teachers cannot help you with a problem if they don't know about it.

lots of good ideas and suggestions. You might develop a signal for when you need a short break, such as holding up two fingers, so that you can go to the water fountain to get a drink. Together you might come up with a reward program to encourage you to remember to raise your hand instead of calling out in class. You and your teacher could find a seat for you in the classroom where you'll have the fewest distractions.

Meeting with your teacher privately would also be a good time to talk about how you can get the homework assignment if you have forgotten to write it down. Maybe your teacher has a classroom website where she posts assignments and upcoming tests and projects. She might also be able to help you select a homework buddy, someone you can call if you aren't sure of an assignment. Also, if you don't

Dora's Strengths and Weaknesses

I created this list of what I'm good at and what's hard for me:

Weaknesses	*Strengths*
I'm messy.	I have great ideas.
I lose things.	I'm a hard worker.
I turn assignments in late.	I can make people laugh.

understand something being taught in class and think you need help, tell your teacher so she can arrange for you to get that extra help from her or a classmate. She might also be able to give your parents a list of tutors if they think that is something that might work for you.

Your parents will probably meet with your teachers (and other professionals at your school) to draw up a plan for your success. You, your teachers, and parents can talk about this plan and decide on accommodations that might help you. Accommodations are tools that make things easier like extra time for testing or a buddy to take class notes for you. Sometimes, the school will set up a special meeting and write up a more official plan that lists all of these helpful tools and aids. These official plans are called Individualized Educational Plans (IEPs) or 504 Accommodation Plans. Big words but these plans are just an organized way to list all of the help you will be getting at school.

Meeting With Your School Counselor

If you have problems with other kids making fun of you at lunch or on the playground or trouble at home (like fighting with your siblings), your school counselor is a good person to talk with, too. (Not all schools have counselors, but if yours does, remember that they can be a great resource.) Try to be as specific as possible when you meet with your counselor and don't be afraid to speak up for yourself. It might be helpful to write out your feelings and questions in advance to help you get exactly what you need from your school counselor. It's important for you to think through what you want to talk about before you meet. It's also important to discuss how things are going at home and with your friends. Your teacher and school counselor have worked with lots of kids. Remember, talking to your school counselor doesn't mean that you're messed up or that you can't handle problems on your own. It shows responsibility and courage.

Attention, Attention!

Here are a few things to keep in mind when talking with adults at school:

- Don't be afraid. Teachers and counselors are there to help you.

- Be specific. Bring in copies of your schoolwork or discuss a behavior that isn't helpful. Sara told her teacher, "I don't like it when you call out my name in front of the class to see if I am on the right page in my science book."

- Point out ways your teacher could help you. Hannah asked her teacher if he could erase the white board more frequently.

Your parents can also talk with your school counselor (and teachers) about how things are going in school like Maddie's parents did. Then you can all agree on a plan to make things go more smoothly for you. Your counselor can also help you and your parents decide if you are having problems compared to other kids your age.

Visiting Your Doctor

Your doctor probably has known you since you were a baby or small child. Your doctor will make sure that you are healthy. He or she can also prescribe medication to help with your AD/HD symptoms if you need it. (We'll talk more about medication in Chapter 5.) When you visit your doctor regularly for check-ups, tell him how you are feeling. Be sure to report any uncomfortable side effects with your medications or other problems that you are having. Your doctor is a great resource for any questions you may have about your AD/HD. He can give you tips on healthy eating, exercise, and can point you to other important people who can be on your support team, like your therapist.

Working With a Therapist

Sometimes, kids with AD/HD might also need to talk with a professional therapist whose job is talking to people about their problems. A therapist can be a social worker, psychologist, or psychiatrist. You might have met with one of them when you were being diagnosed with AD/HD.

Working with a therapist will give you the chance to talk about the many different feelings you have. Since a therapist is outside of your family and school, you can be honest and say what you think. The therapist's job is to listen to you about what is bothering you and to help you figure out what you want to do about it. Remember, the therapist is on your side and ready to help make things easier for you. Because a therapist has had special training and works with many other kids with AD/HD just like you, he can help you deal with your feelings and make a plan for helping things get better in your life. You can work together with your therapist on raising your self-esteem and getting along better with your friends and family, among many other things. Sometimes the therapist meets with your parents to give them some helpful suggestions, too.

> **You can be honest and say what you think.**

Christine Gets Help!

Christine talked to a psychologist about her behaviors and worked out a plan to help her get her behaviors under better control.

- Christine learned about deep breathing to calm herself. She would take deep breaths and count to 10 when something upsetting happened.

- They worked to set up a reward system with her parents for good behavior at home. She earns points towards a new DVD if she uses words instead of just reacting to a situation.

- If Christine forgets to control herself and starts to lose it, her mom calls out "RED LIGHT!"

Getting Extra Help

At times, you may find that you need a little extra help with school-work or with organization. There are other people that can help you catch up and learn some new skills. These professionals are called tutors. A tutor is a person who helps you with your schoolwork. She can come to your house or to your school. She usually helps you with school subjects like math or reading or history. She can also help you learn how to study for tests or with your writing assignments.

Many kids with AD/HD are behind in their schoolwork, not because they aren't smart, but rather because they were not paying attention in class when the teacher taught the skill or material the first time. Your tutor can go over what you have missed and help you with any problems you are now having in school or with homework.

Attention, Attention!

When you meet with your therapist, here are some things you might do together:

- Talk about your feelings or things that are bothering you.

- Draw pictures of your dreams, your family, or your favorite things.

- Play board games to practice good behavior in groups.

- Take tests to see how you learn best.

Sometimes kids even meet with the therapist and a group of other kids instead of one-on-one to talk about feelings and behaviors.

Finding Even More Help

Recently, people called coaches have been working with kids with AD/HD to help them do better. Just like a basketball coach helps you learn skills like shooting and dribbling, an AD/HD coach teaches you skills to get better organized and keep on top of things. She also works with you to find the best way for you to do things and helps you practice these skills until they become easier for you. She can also work with you on setting up goals that you want to achieve (like getting your assignments in on time or keeping your room clean like Dora or not forgetting your books like Frannie). She will then help you break down each goal into small doable steps. It's fun working with a coach because your coach will have lots of ideas about how to do things in ways that fit the way you like to do things. After you have worked with a tutor or coach for a while you will definitely see progress in your grades in school and things will just seem easier.

I hope this chapter has shown you that you don't have to deal with your AD/HD alone! Everyone on your team will work hard to do his or her part in helping you manage your behaviors and achieve success. Just remember that you are the most important part of this team. Your ideas, cooperation, and hard work all add up when it comes to making positive changes in your life. With help and lots of practice and patience, you can reach the finish line and achieve your goals!

Part Two

Take Control of Your AD/HD!

Chapter Four

How Can I Take Control of My Life?

Maddie was glad she had a name for her problems. She was also relieved to know that there was something that she could do about her AD/HD, but she still had questions. How could she possibly improve her attention span, control her other problems, and become more organized? She needed a plan!

Are you forgetful like Frannie or disorganized like Dora? Do you have problems remembering to do your chores or to hang up your coat or pick up your clothes? Do you have trouble following directions or forget when someone asks you to do something that has several parts or steps? Do you forget the rules at home or at school and get into trouble because of it? And what about having trouble with homework? All of these problems combined can make your life feel out of control! But have no fear, there are a lot of things you can do to get back in control. Finding out you have AD/HD is the first step. Here in this chapter, you learn how you can take control and be more successful at home and in school.

To begin, let's take a look at the list of strengths and weaknesses you wrote down earlier. Each of your weaknesses could probably be turned into strengths if you find ways to:

Get organized
Manage your time
Get help with homework
Pay attention and follow directions

For the rest of the chapter, I'll talk about some tips and techniques than can help you turn your weaknesses into strengths. This may seem like a lot of information (it is!), so don't feel like you need to take on everything at once! You might want to work on one skill at a time or just work on a few related ones. When you start to use and master these tips and techniques, everything will become easier to manage!

Getting Organized

Let's talk about some ways to help you get more organized and to keep you from forgetting your home-work assignments, losing your shoes, or leaving your glasses or house keys behind.

HELPFUL TIPS FOR HOME

The first few tips involve working with your parents to set up a program to get you more organized at home. First, you can make a HOME for things. A HOME is the place where a specific object lives. When you're not using it, the object should always be in its HOME. Begin by putting a box or basket near the front door. This is the place to keep all the things that you need for school. That way, when you leave the house in the morning, you won't leave anything that is important behind. These important things might include your backpack, homework, gym shoes, and lunch.

Next, you can create a HOME for your other important stuff. A hook, shelf, or drawer can also be a HOME. Have fun with it! Make a sign like "My Locker Key's HOME!" or "HOME for my hat and mittens!" This way, you can check to see if your things are at HOME where they belong. If not, find them and put them there before

Dora's Organization Tips

These are just a few ways I keep myself organized:

- Use shelves as a HOME to store my stuff, even clothes.

- Use hooks to hang up my pajamas every morning.

- Use baskets and bins for my art supplies.

- Use my favorite color to label my baskets, shelves, and notebooks.

- Put a large calendar and dry-erase board in my room.

- Make every Sunday my day for cleaning up.

you go to bed at night. Now everything has a HOME and you will know just where to find it the next morning when you are leaving for school. You can even create a HOME for other things like your keys, glasses, or anything else that is important to take with you. Use pegs with labels under them or draw an outline of things like tools or craft materials (scissors, tape, or a ruler) on a board attached to the wall of your room to show where each thing goes.

In addition to giving everything a HOME, there are a lot more ways you can get yourself organized at home. Another really helpful tip includes making checklists for routine tasks with multiple steps or for busy days. That might include a checklist for organizing your backpack each night, planning for a sleepover party, or taking care of your bird. The options are limitless!

You can also use a checklist or chart to help you get control over certain behaviors or bad habits. These are usually called "Behavior or Reward Charts." Talk to your parents, teacher, or therapist about a behavior you want to improve, then ask them to help you make up a daily chart to track your progress towards this goal. Each time you act a certain way or remember to do a task, you can earn a check or

Fiona's Birthday Sleepover Checklist

Here's what I'm going to do for my birthday sleepover:

- Create a guest list.
- Decide on snacks with Mom.
- Create party music playlist.
- Organize a clean-up team.
- Send out invitations.
- Order a cake.
- Plan games.

a sticker. When you reach a certain number of checks, you get an agreed upon reward. Reward charts can be fun and will show you the progress you're making towards achieving your goal of a new behavior or skill.

You might also think about making a checklist HOME so you always know where to find all your lists. Use your computer or your PDA to make and track your checklists. Speaking of lists, to-do lists are very helpful, too. If you have a busy day coming up or if you have a tendency to forget things you're supposed to do, making a to-do list can be a real life-saver! Each night before you go to bed, take a few minutes and create a to-do list for the next day. Ask your parents to help you make this list or to remind you to make the list. In the morning and during the day, be sure to check your list to see what you need to do. If you find that you don't get to complete everything on your list that day, just add it to the next day's list when you write it out that night.

A to-do list can be a real life-saver!

Another great way to keep yourself organized at home is to create a message center where you and your family can write and update to-do lists, checklists, schedules, and reminders. This way, you and your family work as a team to help you stay in control and organized. You can even write encouraging notes to one another or you can display things you're proud of, like a great grade on your math test or an award for your service on safety patrol. A white board or cork bulletin board in the kitchen or family room makes a great message center.

SUPER TIPS FOR SCHOOL

Now that we have found some ways to help keep you more organized at home, let's talk about tips to work on special school problems. If you find that you're always losing your important school papers, set up a special folder that stays in your backpack and holds all your important papers, homework, and permission slips. This will be the place to put important papers that you want to get to or from school. Try to get a folder that's your favorite color so you can see it easily. You can mark it TOP PRIORITY and draw a picture or put a photograph of your own home on the front of it. That will make it harder to lose.

Now, do you frequently forget what you have for homework or lose the paper you have written your assignments on? Try using a Special Assignment Place! Select one special place and *only* write your homework assignments there. Don't write them anywhere else! Not on your hand! Not on the back of your test! Not on a gum wrapper! Not on the inside of your book! Some schools give out special assignment books. If yours doesn't, ask your parents to buy one that works for you. A special assignment notebook or assignment sheet in the front of your three-ringed binder can also work well as your Special Assignment Place if you don't have an assignment book. If your school and parents allow it, you might also try using an electronic organizer like a PDA or voice recorder. Some kids can even save their assignments as a note in their cell phones so they have them when they get home. Experiment! Try several of these Special Assignment Places for remembering your homework assignments until you find the one that works best for you.

Experiment!

Managing Your Time

As we talked about in Chapter 1, you probably have problems keeping track of time, like when you're at home playing games for hours, or when you're at school and you run out of time when you're taking a test. Learning to manage your time better by keeping track of time and not putting things off to the last minute will help you stay organized, more relaxed, and in control! Here are some tips to help do just that.

MEASURE TIME

The first step to managing your time is getting a better sense of how long it really takes you to do something. Most kids with AD/HD find that they are not good at judging the passing of time. They either think they can finish a job in a short time, when it actually takes them longer, or they think that a project will take them longer than it actually does. So, how can you get a truer sense of time? Practice!

Let's try. Look at a clock. Now, close your eyes and keep them closed until you think that a minute is up. Now, open your eyes. Were you correct? Next, try to keep your eyes closed for 5 minutes. Ten minutes. Keep playing this game by yourself or get others to do it with you until you have a better sense of time.

Let's try to estimate how long it will take you to complete a homework assignment. On a piece of paper write down how long you think it will take. Look at the clock and begin. When you are finished, look at the clock again. Note the time and write that down on the paper as well. Did they match? Did it take you longer than expected? Accurately estimating how long it will take you to get an assignment done is important for planning how long you need to schedule to do your homework each day.

STOP PROCRASTINATION

Let's talk about procrastination—leaving things for later or putting things off. Procrastination is a problem for some kids with AD/HD because they often like to live "in the now," only thinking about what they want to do at this minute. Maybe you are the same. If something doesn't need to be done now, do you feel that you don't need to do it, that you can wait until later? Do you put things off and wait until the assignment or activity is practically on top of you?

How can you get a truer sense of time? Practice!

Then you may use the pressure of needing to do it now to get it done. You do get things done, but at a cost. You might feel anxious and worry that you won't finish on time.

There is also another cost. The final work that you do at the last minute on a project is often not your best. Ask yourself, "If I had more time, could I have done a better job?" If you answer "yes," you see why it is important to get into a habit to get things done on a schedule and ahead of time rather than leaving them for the last minute. But how can you do that? The best way is to set up a schedule or routine to get things done.

If you establish a routine, you'll have a lot more free time.

SET UP A SCHEDULE

Work with your parent or another adult to set up a schedule for what you need to get done every day or week. Post a list in your room to help you keep on schedule. For each morning and evening, set up a routine time to check your schedule to see what needs to be done. If you establish a routine (start doing the same things at the same time every day), you'll soon find that things will be easier to remember and you'll have a lot more free time to do what you want to do, instead of what you need to do. With a routine you will also find that you are less likely to forget to do something or to put it off until the last minute. All of which will help reduce your anxiety or worry and keep you out of trouble!

BREAK DOWN LONG-TERM ASSIGNMENTS

You can set up a calendar in your room (some kids like to use a white board that they can write on) or in a notebook for your activities or projects. When you get a long-term assignment, the first step is to write the due date on your calendar. Circle the date with your favorite color or in red or put a colorful sticker on it. Then work backwards on

Tatiana's Super Schedule!

Here is what I do every Monday:

7:00 am	Wake up/shower/dress/eat breakfast
7:45 am	Catch school bus
3:00 pm	Go home!
3:30 pm	Eat a snack
4–6:00 pm	Do my homework
6:15 pm	Have dinner!
7–7:30 pm	Finish chores/help with dishes/feed Byron
7:30–8:00 pm	Take a shower/brush teeth
8–9:00 pm	Watch my favorite TV shows
9:00 pm	Make lunch/check backpack/set out clothes for school tomorrow
9:30 pm	Go to bed!

When you finish, reward yourself!

your calendar to break the task down into smaller, more doable parts (you may need to work with your parent, teacher, or tutor to do this part). Each part of the project should have its own separate due date. Try to set up your schedule to see if you can even finish a little ahead of the due date. That will give you the opportunity to check over your work or ask for help if you need it. It will also take the pressure off of you to get things done in a hurry, creating more stress and anxiety. When you finish, reward yourself with something special like a pizza for dinner or extra time outside or a movie with your friends. Your parents will be glad to help you plan your reward as they see you taking more responsibility and getting your work done on time.

REMEMBER TESTS AND ASSIGNMENTS

Another way to manage your assignments and tests is to set up a program with your teachers to remind you when a long-term assignment or project is due or when you will have a test. You may forget about these important projects or tests that don't happen every day as part of your school routine. Lots of schools now have e-mail. If yours does, ask your teachers if they would please e-mail your assignment and test schedules to you or your mom or dad so that you can print them out and put them in your calendar. Or maybe they can mail a copy of the instructions and due dates for all your long-term assignments to your home. Your mom or dad could give each of them a set of stamped, addressed envelopes for this and then all they will need to do is put a copy in the envelope and drop it in the mail. That way you will have an extra copy at home in case you lose the instructions and due dates you get in class.

Getting Help With Homework

Now let's tackle some homework problems, like forgetting your books or your assignments, that kids with AD/HD like Frannie might have. We covered some tips earlier in the chapter, but here are some more that can really help. Work with your teacher to set up a program at school to make sure you have the correct books for your homework each night. Perhaps your teacher can check your backpack to see that you have your books. If forgetting a book becomes a big problem, you might try bringing home all of your books every night or have your parents talk with your teacher about keeping an extra set of books at home.

HOMEWORK BUDDY

Homework buddies help each other out in school and check that each has what they need to do their homework. A homework buddy

Fiona's Project Schedule

Here's the schedule for my history essay project:

Mon	Decide on topic.
Tues	Research topic at library and online.
Wed	Take notes from research.
Thurs	Create timeline and outline for essay.
Sat	Write essay.
Mon	Hand in rough draft of essay.
Tues	Make corrections on draft and finish the essay.
Wed	Hand in final essay.

is also someone that you can contact to check on what you have for homework or to ask what you need to bring in to school the next day. Your homework buddy should be organized and should get good grades in school.

But how do you go about getting a homework buddy? If there is someone you want to work with, ask that person if you can be homework buddies. If you don't want to ask someone yourself, your teacher can help you find someone. To make these arrangements, you can talk to that person at school and get his or her phone number or e-mail address, but be sure to have your mom or dad call his or her parent to make sure it's okay for you to call in the evenings. Every so often you could do something nice for your homework buddy. You might offer to take him or her to the movies or for an ice cream as a way of thanking him or her for helping you.

STUDYING STRATEGIES

Now that you have a system set up to help you remember your books, what your homework assignment is and when it is due, let's talk about finding a time and space to do it in. First, it is important to find out where and when you work best. Some questions to ask when thinking about where and when to study are: Do you like to work on your homework as soon as you get home or do you like to have a snack and rest and get started after dinner? Do you work best alone or if someone is in the room to keep you on track? Do you like it quiet or do you work best with music in the background?

After thinking about the answers to these questions for a while, it is important to discuss them with your parents. Maybe you'll even need to try doing your homework in various places or at different times to discover what works best for you. Once you have found the best place and time for you, always try to do your homework there. It will become a routine and you'll be less likely to be distracted and will get more work done.

Some girls who have trouble sitting still like Hannah seem to study better if they work in short spurts. Scheduling regular study breaks for a snack or to get up and walk around can also help you concentrate better and get more done. Hannah has discovered that if she works for 15 or 20 minutes and then gets up for a 5-minute break, she gets more done. If you try this tip, be sure to set a timer or look at a clock to stay on schedule. Fiona learned that when she exercised before settling down to study, she could focus better and longer.

Some kids say that they need to be alone to work or study, but many have said that they need to be near others. Some girls seem to like having someone else in the room to keep them on track while they study. Having a parent or

> Scheduling regular study breaks can help you concentrate better and get more done.

a babysitter sit quietly in the room may be all that you need to get your work done. That person can just be there in case you need help and can also provide the "brakes" to prevent you from getting up and playing with other toys, doodling, or staring off into space for long periods. Gentle reminders and words of encouragement from them can go a long way to helping you stay on task. The important point is that the person is not there to help or to talk, but to just "keep you company."

Paying Attention and Following Directions

Now that we've started to work on getting you more organized, let's work on two other problems that kids with AD/HD have: paying attention and following directions. If you don't pay attention, you can loose track of your things, miss important instructions from your teacher, and just plain feel out of sorts. And if you can't follow directions and rules, how do you expect to get and stay organized? After all, being organized involves following rules that you've made for yourself, like you have to put your coat in the closet every time you come home. Let's take a look at a really cool technique that can help you improve your attention and follow directions.

One of the best ways to remember what someone is saying to you is to use more than just your ears to listen. By engaging your brain, and using your eyes, ears, and mouth, you'll become a much better listener. The **STOP! LOOK! LISTEN! and REPEAT!** system helps you do just that! Many kids with AD/HD have difficulty following directions. Usually, it's because they were not paying attention or were distracted by something else when the directions were given the first

time. This can happen both at home when your parents ask you to do something or at school when the teacher gives you directions in class.

The **STOP! LOOK! LISTEN! and REPEAT!** system means just what it says. When someone is talking to you or giving you directions, you **STOP** what you are doing (playing a game, watching TV, or daydreaming) and engage your brain by paying attention. Next you **LOOK** at them (in the eyes or at their mouth is the best), and you really **LISTEN**. That means that you actively show that you know what they are saying by nodding, saying "OK" or "Yeah." You then **REPEAT** what you have heard or what they have asked you to do: "You mean you want me to get my sweater off the floor in the hallway right now, put it in the closet, and then set the table for dinner," or "Are you saying that I can play with my friends at Aysha's house for an hour, but then I have to come home?"

If you are not exactly sure what someone is asking you to do or how you should do it at the **LISTEN** stage, it is the perfect time to ask questions and go over it with them until you completely understand what is expected of you. For example, "How will I know when an hour is up? Will you call me to remind me or shall I ask Aysha's mother to tell me when it is 5 o'clock and I have to go home? Okay, I got it now. I'll tell Aysha's mother when I get there that I can only stay an hour and ask her to remind me. I'll be home a little after 5."

> When the teacher gives you directions, you can use the STOP! LOOK! LISTEN! and REPEAT! system.

When the teacher gives you directions or homework assignments in class, you can also use the **STOP! LOOK! LISTEN! and REPEAT!** system. Remember, first you must **STOP** what you are doing and

Listen! Repeat!

Christine's **STOP! LOOK! LISTEN! and REPEAT!** Reminders

Here's how I remember the **STOP! LOOK! LISTEN! and REPEAT!** system:

- I taped a little red stop sign to my desk.

- I printed "STOP" on a piece of paper in big red letters and attached it to my desk and the cover of my notebook.

- I created a signal word with my parents and teacher. When they say that word, I **STOP** what I'm doing, **LOOK**, and **LISTEN** to them.

LOOK at the teacher or **LOOK** at the directions she is writing on the board or **LOOK** at the directions written on the paper in front of you. Then you need to actively **LISTEN** by nodding your head silently or writing down what your teacher is saying. If the directions are written in front of you on the paper or test, you can underline or highlight the important parts as your teacher is talking. This is the same as **REPEATING** them aloud. If you don't understand, now is the time to raise your hand and ask a question to make it clearer.

Right now, you're probably thinking, "This sounds great, but how will I ever remember to use the **STOP! LOOK! LISTEN! and REPEAT!** system?" Can you think of some other ways you can remember to use this system? Brainstorm and see what you come up with. Be sure to discuss the **STOP! LOOK! LISTEN! and REPEAT!** system with your parents and teachers. Maybe they will have some other good ideas that can help you, too. They can also help you remember to use it by giving you a signal or by saying, **"STOP! LOOK! LISTEN! and REPEAT!"**

Remember that members of your support team (we talked about them in Chapter 3) can help you get and stay organized, too! Your parents, teachers, school counselor, tutors, and coaches are there to support you! And now that we have gotten things running a little more smoothly for you at home and at school, let's talk about taking medication to help your AD/HD and learning more about yourself as you adjust to managing your attention disorder.

Chapter Five

Will Medicine Help Me With My AD/HD?

Maddie used several of the tips that her teacher and tutor suggested and she did get more organized, but no matter how hard she tried, Maddie still found it nearly impossible to pay attention for very long. When she and her mother visited Dr. Shaw, they told him about this continuing problem. At that visit, Dr. Shaw suggested that Maddie try a medicine that could improve her attention span and help her pay better attention.

What if no matter how hard you try, it's still impossible to consistently pay attention, follow directions, get your work done, or sit still? What should you do if you or a support team member thinks that you might need extra help staying focus and organized and suggests that medication may help you?

Some kids are able to use Behavior or Reward Charts (Remember these from Chapter 4?) and other supportive programs to keep their AD/HD behaviors in check. But like Maddie, some other kids (and adults, too) take medication for their AD/HD.

For them in addition to organization and behavior strategies, tips, and tools, like those listed in this book, medication reduces the

behaviors of AD/HD and is part of the overall plan to make things better. Let's take a closer look at these medications, and what and who can help you learn if medication is right for you.

Knowing If You Need Medication

After your diagnosis and working on your action plan for several weeks, you might still feel like things aren't getting better or a support team member (like your parents, teacher, or tutor) might notice that you're still having problems. If so, it's probably time to reevaluate your plan and consider taking medication for your AD/HD.

Before making this decision, you'll need to talk with your parents and let them know about the problems you're still having and how hard things are for you. Your support team member (teacher or tutor) might also be involved in this discussion. Don't be afraid to have this conversation with your parents. They are there to help!

At this point, you and your parents may decide to talk with your doctor or psychiatrist to find out if taking medication can help you get your AD/HD under control. In this meeting, get as much information as you can. Talk to your doctor about what changes might happen and what you should expect from the medication. Ask your doctor about the benefits (and possible side effects) of medication. Don't be afraid to ask your doctor about other options you might have. And tell your doctor how you might feel when taking medication, or if anything else is bothering you. It's good for you to ask lots of questions and read books about medication and AD/HD before

Maddie's Doctor Tips

My mom told me that no question is too silly, so when I talked with my doctor, I asked:

- What is the name of my medicine?

- When should I take it?

- How long will it last? Will I need to take it more than once a day?

- Are there any side effects?

- Will the medicine make me feel "different" or "funny?"

- How will it taste?

you start medication. But, if you feel a little shy about this, your parents can ask questions and help, too. Remember, taking medication for AD/HD doesn't mean that you are sick, that your AD/HD is worse than other kids with AD/HD who don't need medication, or that you are a failure. It just means that you need a little more help to make things better for you.

It's important to know that medications for AD/HD don't make you smarter or directly control your feelings or behaviors. And medication won't magically take care of everything. You'll still need to use other strategies and skills to stay organized and focused. The medications simply help you to be more in control and allow you to focus on learning new skills and ways of behaving. You may not even notice you are taking medicine, except that things are not so frustrating for you anymore. AD/HD cannot be cured, but it can be managed with help.

After talking with your doctor and getting all of your questions answered, only you and your parents can decide if medication is right for you. It's very important for you and your parents to understand the medication and its effects and to make your decision based on facts and information gathered from your doctor. It's also a great chance to really think about how you feel about taking medication for your AD/HD and to have your parents and doctor help your sort though your feelings about this. That way you can really feel "in-charge" of the situation, and that's a good thing!

> **Medication won't magically take care of everything.**

> **Only you and your parents can decide if medication is right for you.**

Finding the Right Medication

Each kid with AD/HD is unique. That means that certain medications are better at reducing the behaviors associated with AD/HD for some kids than for others. Today there are many medications used to treat AD/HD. Your doctor will have lots of medications to choose from to help lessen the impact of AD/HD in your day-to-day life. Sometimes it may take a while to find the right medication to help you do better in school, at home, and with friends. So don't get discouraged if you need to try a few medicines before you find the one that's right for you.

Each year, new medications for AD/HD are being made. Some may last longer and some may work better for you. Having different medicines gives you more options. A medicine that works well for you might not work for someone else. It is not unusual that your medicine may need to be adjusted at times, sometimes a little more, sometimes a little less. Be sure to let your parents and doctor know if you don't think your medicine is working as well as it had been. If you're embarrassed about taking your medication in front of other kids at school, tell your doctor. She may be able to change you to a medication that you only need to take once a day in the morning at home.

Over time, your AD/HD may improve, but it's important to continue to work with your doctor so that you always receive the best treatment to keep things running smoothly.

Medications and What They Do

For some kids with AD/HD, the doctor may prescribe a stimulant medication to help with attention problems. Stimulants are the most common medications used to treat AD/HD. They work by increasing the levels of the neurotransmitters in the synapse and make the brain work better, just like when you use DSL or cable to get a stronger, faster signal on the Internet. (Do you remember talking about these ideas about how the brain works in Chapter 1?)

Don't get discouraged if you need to try a few medicines.

Stimulants can increase your attention span and decrease distractibility. They can also make you less likely to act impulsively (without thinking) and help you to focus on what you need to be doing. Scientists have done lots of studies that prove that these stimulants are both a safe and successful way to treat AD/HD when used correctly. Non-stimulant medications are also used to treat AD/HD. Non-stimulants act a little differently than the stimulants do on the chemicals in the brain but still improve attention and focus.

There are different types of medications used to treat AD/HD, and they include both stimulants and non-stimulants. These medicines are classified by how long they last. They're called:

Short-acting medications
Intermediate-acting medications
Long-acting medications

Your doctor, along with input from you and your parents, will determine which one is right for you, depending on how long you need it to work. Let's take a closer look at each type.

SHORT-ACTING MEDICATIONS
Short-acting medications are usually stimulants that last about 4 to 6 hours. Because their effects don't last very long, you may need to take a pill several times a day in order to improve your attention span for the entire school day. You may also need to take another pill after school for homework and other activities. Your doctor will decide what the best schedule is for you.

INTERMEDIATE-ACTING MEDICATIONS
These medications last a little longer than short-acting medications, maybe 8 to 10 hours. You probably won't need to take another pill

at lunchtime if you take one in the morning. But some kids do need to take another dose in the late afternoon depending on their schedule and behaviors at home. You, your doctor, and your parents will determine this together.

Some of these medications are in capsules that contain small beads that release the medicine more slowly. Some of these capsules can be opened and you can sprinkle the beads on food if you have trouble swallowing a pill. But before you do this, be sure to ask your doctor if it's okay.

LONG-ACTING MEDICATIONS

These medications last the longest, usually at least 12 hours. With these medicines, you only need to take one pill or put on a patch (like a Band-Aid®) in the morning. These pills or patches work all day and into the evening because the medicine releases slowly. All of these medicines have been tested. Studies show that when kids take them they pay attention better and don't have as many behavior problems. They can also do more math problems and get more problems correct than kids with AD/HD who don't take medication. These long-acting medicines may be stimulants or non-stimulants.

Side Effects

Side effects are minor problems that people sometimes get when they take a medicine. The most common side effects of the stimulant medicines used to treat AD/HD are the following:

- Feeling less hungry
- Having problems falling asleep
- Getting headaches or stomachaches
- Becoming more irritable
- Feeling sad a lot of the time

- Feeling too sleepy during the day or when the medicine wears off

Most of these side effects, if they do occur, usually last for only the first few days or weeks that you take these medicines. However, if these problems are severe, don't go away, or get worse while you are taking your medicine, be sure to tell your parents and your doctor. Your doctor can usually help decrease side effects by lowering the amount of medicine you take, changing the schedule of when you take your medicine, or switching to another medication.

Maddie's Tips on Side Effects

At first, I got stomachaches from my medicine, but I dealt with these side effects. Eating healthy foods helped a lot. Here's what else I did:

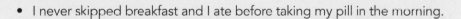

- I never skipped breakfast and I ate before taking my pill in the morning.

- For lunch, I asked my parents to fill my lunch box with my favorite foods (and they always remembered my most favorite healthy ones!).

- When I got home from school, I would grab a piece of fruit or have some yogurt as a snack. Or if I was really hungry, I asked for early dinner.

- In case I got a stomachache during the day at school, and it wasn't lunchtime, I got permission from my teachers to munch on some crackers during class or between periods.

Swallowing Medicine

Swallowing a pill can be difficult or feel weird to some people. Even adults have problems swallowing pills. But it can be a lot easier if you use a few tricks. Usually people get the hang of swallowing a pill after a little practice. Have you ever swallowed gum or a large mouthful of water or other drink? You can practice by putting your pill, a Tic Tac®, or another small candy on the back of your tongue. Fill your mouth and cheeks with water. Hold it for a few seconds with your chin down (don't tilt your head back, the pill will hit the back of your throat). Swallow everything in one big gulping motion. Pill gone!

If after practicing you still have trouble swallowing a pill, some of the stimulant medications for AD/HD are now available as patches (that look kind of like a Band-Aid®) or can be opened and sprinkled into food. Ask your doctor about taking one of these medications, so you don't have to swallow a pill.

Attention, Attention!

Here are a few tricks to swallowing a pill:

- Put the pill in your mouth and then drink a glass of water through a straw. That way you'll concentrate on the straw and won't think about the pill.

- Put the pill in your mouth and then add a spoonful of applesauce, yogurt, or pudding. Then swallow everything all together.

- Chew on a piece of bread or a cookie and then put the pill in your mouth just before you swallow.

Not all kids with AD/HD need to take medication for their AD/HD, but it can be a very important part of your overall plan for success. Some parents and kids might be nervous about adding medications to their action plan because they don't know a lot about them. It is important for you and your parents to keep an open mind and to get all of the facts about these medications. Talking about them with your doctor is very important, as is reading about them. It's also helpful for you to discuss the possibility of taking medication with other kids who already take these medicines. Your parents can talk with the parents of these kids as well. Just remember that medication can be a very good way to treat your AD/HD, but it's not a cure! It's only one part of a larger plan. You still have to make sure you do your part in managing your behaviors.

Chapter Six

Who Should I Tell That I Have AD/HD?

Maddie was happy that things were finally getting better. Some people like her teacher and the school counselor knew that she had AD/HD and it was great to be able to talk with them when she had problems or questions. But Maddie didn't know who else she should tell or talk with about having AD/HD. Could she talk with her grandmother about it? What about the bus driver? Or her basketball coach? Or her friends?

Like Maddie and many other girls recently diagnosed with AD/HD, getting used to the idea that you have AD/HD takes some time. You probably have lots of feelings because of your AD/HD and you will need to sort those out. (We will talk about all of that later on in Chapter 8.) In this chapter, we'll talk about sharing the fact that you have AD/HD and the information you have learned about it and yourself with other people.

Girls with AD/HD often ask, "Can I talk to my friends about my AD/HD? Or should I just talk to my family and doctor about it?" One way to decide if it is important to tell another person about your AD/HD is to ask yourself the question, "Does this person need to know that I have AD/HD in order to help me?" Asking this question will allow you, in most cases, to decide who you will need to tell.

Your parents, doctor, and teacher (and maybe your school counselor) already all know that you have AD/HD. They are probably part of the support team that helped find out why you were having problems and have worked to help make things better. They are your #1 supporters!

Deciding Who to Tell

Girls with AD/HD have many other people in their lives that they see a lot. These people include:

Grandparents and other relatives
Babysitters
Coaches
Camp counselors
Neighbors
Family friends
People at church or synagogue

Your parents most likely have discussed your AD/HD with your relatives and babysitters. It also may be important for coaches and camp counselors to know you have AD/HD in case you need to take your medicine at practice or camp. Your parents will fill out forms before you attend camp and give permission for you to take your medicine. Your athletic team coaches might also need to know your symptoms of

Ask yourself, "Does this person need to know that I have AD/HD?"

Attention, Attention!

Someone may need to know about your AD/HD . . .

- In an emergency or if you are sick or need to go to the hospital.

- If you've forgotten to take your medicine when you're away from home.

- When someone besides your parent supervises you when you take your medicine.

AD/HD and how to best deal with them so that they can make sure that you are paying attention and following the rules at practice or during games. You and your coach can even come up with a special signal for you if they see that you are losing concentration.

It's important that you talk to your parents about who you can talk to about your AD/HD and who they have told. That way you will know ahead of time before talking with neighbors or family friends. Neighbors most likely don't need to know that you have AD/HD, unless you and your family are really good friends with them. Whoever you and your parents choose to tell about your AD/HD, remind those people to respect your privacy and ask them not to discuss or tell other people who really don't need to know about your AD/HD.

Informing Your Support Team Members

At school, in addition to your teachers, there are probably other people on and off your support team that you often see:

School nurse
Lunch room or playground monitor

Girls' Talking Tips on Who to Tell!

Here's what we covered when we talked to our parents about who to tell:

- I asked about who they'd already told.

- I asked my parents to talk with someone that hadn't been told for me.

- We talked about which friends they thought it was okay to tell.

- When my parents thought that I shouldn't tell someone, I asked them why.

- We rehearsed how to answer questions about my AD/HD by role-playing. My parents pretended they were my friends or other people I know.

School bus driver
Guidance counselor

The nurse is a good friend to have at school. Nurses know a lot about AD/HD and the medications used to treat it. If you ever have questions about or problems with AD/HD while at school, you can always ask to visit the nurse to talk. The lunch room and playground monitors and school bus driver probably don't need to know that you have AD/HD. But if you have problems in the lunch room, on the playground, or on the bus, be sure to speak up for yourself and tell an adult who is present. You can also move nearer to the adult monitor on the playground or change your seat on the bus to be closer to the driver. Having your friends stand or sit near you may also help. Also, be sure to discuss any problems with your parents so that they can talk with adults at school to help you.

Telling Your Friends (or Not)

Most of your friends don't need to know that you have AD/HD. You may want to talk about your AD/HD with only a few close friends. That's your decision. Some girls have found that when they do share about their AD/HD and its treatment, their friends are very supportive and helpful, even reminding them to take their medicine on time.

You've probably had close friends that have their own problems like allergies or learning disabilities, and they have talked to you about them. Sometimes sharing this information with a friend makes you closer and better able to understand and help that friend. Talking about your AD/HD could do the same for you. Remember that you can always ask the friends you do tell about your AD/HD to keep it to themselves and to not tell others.

Getting help in school may be another reason to let your friend or homework buddy know that you have AD/HD. That way, they'll know that your AD/HD sometimes makes it hard for you to remember homework assignments, projects, or test dates.

Most of your friends don't need to know that you have AD/HD.

Having AD/HD is an explanation and never an excuse for your behavior.

Using Excuses (Not!)

Telling someone you have AD/HD explains why you might behave in a certain way or have the problems you do, but no one wants to hear a bunch of excuses. Having AD/HD is an explanation and never an excuse for your behavior. If something goes wrong, your AD/HD might be the reason why this happened, but it should not be an excuse for the problem. It is important to do all that you can to take control of your AD/HD and your behaviors. This might include taking your medication, working with teachers, tutors, and others, and tackling your other problems.

Having AD/HD is not something to be ashamed of. Nothing you or your parents have done caused your AD/HD. Remember, it's inherited! Instead, you should feel proud of all you have done and how hard you are working to control your AD/HD and make your life better. So don't be afraid to talk to other people or to ask for help. You might be surprised to find out that other kids also have the same or similar problems and that by speaking up you have helped them.

Part Three

Overcome Your Challenges!

Chapter Seven

How Can I Feel Better About Me?

Maddie was doing much better, but still she was puzzled. On days when she took medication for her AD/HD, she no longer had problems following directions or paying attention, but she still didn't feel as smart as her friends. When she didn't take her medication, her mind would wander and she often forgot to do her chores at home. Who was the real Maddie? The girl she was before she knew she had AD/HD? The one who is now doing so much better in school? Or the one who still messes up on the weekend?

Girls with AD/HD often ask, "Who is the real me?" Is it the girl who was disorganized and forgetful before she started making lists or is it the girl who now knows where her keys and books are? Dora knows that she still has AD/HD and that if she stops making her lists and using the organizing tips that she learned from her tutor, she will go back to being "Disorganized Dora." And Maddie wonders, "Am I the girl who can sit still and pay attention when taking my medication or the one who has more problems when she isn't taking medication? Or am I both?" It might even feel like there are two of you: the AD/HD you and the non-AD/HD you. You're not alone! Lots of kids with AD/HD feel like this!

The key to answering the riddle of "who is the real me?" can be found by looking at AD/HD itself. It is important that you understand that AD/HD cannot be cured like strep throat or a cold and that it doesn't go away. AD/HD is part of who you are. So the "real me" is the one with AD/HD.

Even though it is always there, your AD/HD doesn't have to get in the way of your being successful and having fun. You need to learn to control it instead of having it control who you are. Everyone has to learn to control themselves and work hard to focus on their strengths. Even kids (and grown-ups) without AD/HD!

If you don't take your medicine or use tips like your lists and the **STOP! LOOK! LISTEN! and REPEAT!** system to keep your AD/HD under control, you will see all of your old AD/HD behaviors getting in the way again. If you don't like the fact that all your AD/HD behaviors return when your medication wears off, talk with your parents and doctor. When you control your AD/HD and things are going better for you, you can feel proud knowing you are in charge and in control!

Despite all of this success, many girls with AD/HD like Maddie don't see themselves any differently after their diagnosis and treatment. They still feel like that out-of-control or disorganized or forgetful girl with AD/HD. They continue to see themselves just like before even though they are now doing so much better. Girls might still think that they're stupid, different than everybody else, not popular and have no friends, messing up all the time, or just not able to do anything right. These statements are part of a negative self-talk cycle and poor self-image that girls with AD/HD get locked into. So how can a girl with AD/HD change how she thinks about herself, change her self-image, or raise her self-esteem once things are under control and getting better?

Finding Your Self-Esteem

Self-esteem (or self-concept) is what we think and feel about ourselves. Girls with AD/HD often feel badly about themselves because of the problems they have had. They might think that they are not very smart or feel different than other girls. They might think that other people only see them with the problems they used to have. When a girl feels badly about herself, we say she has low self-esteem. How can you tell if you have low self-esteem? Let's look at girls with high and low self-esteem.

Girls with high self-esteem usually:

- Feel good about themselves
- Are usually happy or in a good mood
- Enjoy their friends
- Feel sure of themselves
- Can say "no" to peer pressure
- Look others in the eye when they talk with them
- Are aware of their strengths and weaknesses
- Are proud of their success
- Can accept criticism and compliments
- Can laugh at themselves
- Learn from their mistakes
- Are willing to try new things

- Can play by themselves
- Take pride in their appearance and dress neatly

Girls with low self-esteem may have some of these problems:

- Frequently complain about things
- Always notice things that they think are wrong about themselves
- Feel that they mess up a lot
- Have a negative attitude
- Have trouble making and keeping friends
- Need to be liked by everyone
- Put themselves down
- Feel they are not as smart as others
- Are critical of others
- Blame others for their mistakes
- Have difficulty accepting praise
- Take criticism poorly
- Get frustrated easily
- Usually quit before they give something a chance
- Make up stories about themselves and what they have done
- Can be messy or not care about how they look

Talk to your family and friends about how you can make yourself feel better.

Boosting Your Self-Esteem

After looking at these lists, you might find that you need a boost in self-esteem. How can you boost your self-esteem? You can always talk to your friends and family about ideas for how they make themselves feel better. To get you started, here are some ideas.

POSITIVE MENTAL ATTITUDE

Having a positive mental attitude means being proud of yourself and looking at your strengths rather than dwelling on your weaknesses.

One way to develop your positive mental attitude is to learn to laugh at yourself and don't be afraid of making mistakes. Low self-esteem can make it harder for you to take a chance and try an activity. Instead of trying, you become a quitter. Remember, nobody is perfect and everybody makes mistakes. That often is the best way to learn. Also, learn to accept criticism and make good use of it. Nobody starts out good at everything. Try to think about how you can use the criticism to help improve what you are doing.

Saying "thank you" when you receive a compliment and feeling good about receiving it will really boost your self-esteem. Compliment others. It will make you feel better. Always speak to others as you would like them to speak to you. When you're kind to others, they'll be kind to you in return!

Another way to build a positive mental attitude is to start taking care of yourself at home. You'll feel more grown up and in control of your life. This might mean keeping your room clean, washing your own clothes or dishes, or making your own lunch for school. Ask your mom to let you help out in the kitchen. Maybe your mom or dad can even teach you to make a few simple meals like a grilled cheese sandwich, pizza, or salad. Using the microwave can be a safe and easy way for you to learn to prepare meals. As you learn new skills and feel more in charge, you'll feel better about yourself.

To feel good about yourself, walk with confidence. That means having good posture, holding your head up high, and making good eye contact (looking at others directly in the eyes). You'll find that you look and eventually will feel more confident.

POSITIVE SELF-TALK

By breaking the negative self-talk cycle, you can really boost your self-esteem. You can do this by changing how you talk to yourself. Instead of saying "Nobody likes me" or "I always mess up" or

Learn to laugh at yourself!

Samantha's Confidence Builders!

I wanted to change "Shy Sam" into "Self-confident Sam." So here are some ways I found that built my confidence. I learned to:

- Express myself in words.

- Speak clearly.

- Always stick up for myself and know that what I think is right.

- Find things that I am good at and do them.

- Accept that everybody is different.

- Set small goals and try to meet them.

It's hard, but I just keep trying and never give up. You can do it, too!

"I can't," try saying things that give you courage or make you feel better. Instead of saying something negative, try saying something positive. You could say something like, "I CAN do this!" or even "Maybe I'm not good in spelling, but I am great in art."

Making a list of things about yourself that you are proud of is a great way to jump-start your positive self-talk cycle. Keep this list somewhere special, like on your bulletin board in your room or on your bedside table, so that you can look at it when you start to get down on yourself. And remember to keep adding to the list!

HOBBIES AND EXERCISE

You can also build self-esteem by finding an area or a hobby that you are good at and have fun doing. This might be dancing, singing, acting in a play, or taking care of a pet. If you are a good reader, you may find you feel better after reading stories to some of the younger kids that you know. You might even want to exercise or play a sport. Just get moving! You will feel better. If you are not interested in team sports, try an activity like swimming, skating, diving, horseback riding, or biking.

Remember to keep and value your old friends.

FRIENDS!

Friends are a great way to boost your self-esteem. Look for friends who have high self-esteem and feel good about themselves. Make new friends, but remember to keep and value your old friends. They are the ones who know all about you and like you for who you are. Friends, whether new or old, can help you learn ways to look at yourself more positively.

You have already taken a very big step to building self-esteem and changing your life by reading this book. You probably were a little resistant when your parents bought this book for you. But by being open to finding out the truth about yourself and learning ways to manage your AD/HD, you have taken control and broken the negative self-talk cycle. In no time, you'll be the expert on YOU and will be able to recognize when things are going well or when you need to ask for help. You should already feel proud and more confident about yourself!

Chapter Eight

How Do I Deal With My Feelings?

When Maddie looked back over the last few months, she felt like she had been on a roller coaster ride. She had experienced a lot of different feelings in a short time. She had been worried, confused, scared, puzzled, and relieved. Even now, she continued to feel misunderstood and sad and discouraged at times when things were not going well. What could she do with all of these feelings? Who should she talk with about them?

> It may take time for things to get better and you will still have some bad days.

Girls with AD/HD are often very sensitive and have many strong feelings because things have been difficult for them both at home and at school. It is important for you to deal with the feelings and confusion that have built up over the years that you didn't know you had AD/HD. Even after you are diagnosed, you need to understand that it may take time for things to get better and you will still have some bad days. Be willing to give yourself a break, laugh at your mistakes, and take time to build up your self-esteem by trying some of the things we discussed in the last chapter. In this chapter, let's spend some time talking about some of your feelings. Remember, all kids have these feelings, so you're not alone!

Feeling Discouraged

If you're always in trouble or getting yelled at because of your AD/HD, it would be easy to become discouraged and unhappy. Sometimes girls with AD/HD get discouraged if things keep going wrong no matter how hard they try like Dora. Others become sad and cry over the littlest things like Christine.

Don't be discouraged! Getting help from others and learning more about AD/HD will make it easier for you. Be assured that things will get better over time. Now that you are diagnosed, you know what the problem is, and you can begin working on a plan to deal with your AD/HD symptoms and feel more in control just like Christine.

Not Feeling So Smart

Having problems in school or with homework may make you feel that you're not as smart as other kids. Kids with AD/HD are usually just as smart as

Give
yourself
a break!

other kids (or sometimes smarter!). Talking with your teacher about what you are finding difficult is an important step to making school easier. Teachers are always willing to help and spend a little more time explaining things to you if you don't understand. The time management techniques and other strategies we talked about in Chapter 4 will also help. If a particular project or assignment is difficult for you, try setting up some time to work with your homework buddy, friend, or older brother or sister, especially if they are good in that subject. If you have problems with organization or real problems in learning to read, write, or do math, maybe it's time to talk to your parents about getting a tutor or a coach. Working on building your self-esteem (as talked about in Chapter 7) will definitely help too. A little self-esteem boost goes a long way!

Feeling Lonely and Misunderstood

Not having friends can make you feel lonely and sad like Samantha, who is shy, or Caroline, who is so bossy even though she doesn't

Don't Feel So Lonely!

Here's how we keep ourselves busy so we don't feel so lonely:

- I got a pet. Taking care of my puppy keeps me plenty busy!

- I joined a group, singing in the school chorus.

- I took up a hobby, skateboarding!

- I acted in a play with our local theater group.

- I volunteer for community service with my family.

mean to be. You may feel picked on or misunderstood because even when you try to do the right thing, you still might make mistakes. This is how Fiona felt when she was told to stop humming and she didn't even know she was doing it. This can all be very confusing. But there are ways you can deal with these feelings. You could keep a journal of your thoughts and feelings and then share them with your parents, school counselor, teacher, or other member of your support team. That way, they'll understand why you feel or act the way you do. You might also read a book or watch a movie about kids who feel lonely or misunderstood and see how they triumph! Another way to not feel lonely is to work on your friendship skills! We'll talk about that in the next chapter.

Attention, Attention!

Here are some great books about "misunderstood" kids triumphing! Go to the library or your local bookstore for even more books!

- *Charlie and the Chocolate Factory* by Roald Dahl

- *Tales of a Fourth Grade Nothing* by Judy Blume

- *Diary of a Wimpy Kid* by Jeff Kinney

- *Harriet the Spy* by Louise Fitzhugh

- *The Tale of Despereaux* by Kate Dicamillo

- *Ella Enchanted* by Gail Carson Levine

Tatiana's Plan for Taming Her Anger and Frustration

Here's what I do when I need to control my anger or frustration:

- Watch for anger warning signs. (Clenched fists? Hot face? Louder voice?)

- Take a deep breath and relax.

- Use my words to talk out my feelings.

- Count to 10.

- Tell the other person I'm getting angry or frustrated.

- Ask for a break. Then I come back later when I'm calm to talk things over or try again.

- I might just sleep on it.

Feeling Angry and Frustrated

Anger and frustration are very normal feelings that result when things are not going well. It's okay and natural to feel angry at these times, but it is NOT okay to act on these feelings. Girls with AD/HD often get frustrated when they cannot complete a task or assignment quickly. They get angry at themselves or others when they are stressed or feeling picked on or misunderstood. The first step in controlling anger is to look at what makes you angry or frustrated and develop a plan to deal with it. Uncontrolled anger is like a wild tiger, but it can be tamed. Becoming aware of what makes you

Maddie's Tips on Talking About Feelings

Here are some ideas for when you talk to your parents. They helped me!

- Just do it! It gets easier the more you talk.

- Practice what you want to say.

- Have courage and be honest.

- Stick up for yourself. Don't let others tell you how you are feeling.

- Only say what you are feeling, not what you think others are feeling.

- Use "I" statements like "I feel silly" instead of "She thinks I'm silly."

angry will allow you to anticipate angry feelings that might come up in a specific situation and allow you a little space and time to calm down. Of course, the best strategy is to avoid those situations all together (just like you would a tiger), but since that usually is impossible, you definitely need a plan.

One thing you should do when you get upset is to find out what makes you angry or frustrated. Make a list of these "trigger points," situations that get you upset. You can then concentrate on avoiding your "trigger points." You might also work on recognizing the early signs of anger. Your breathing might speed up, your face might get hot, or you might begin sweating. If you get really upset or frustrated, take a time out. Give yourself a break and walk away from the situation that's upsetting you. Remember, you can always get back in control by using some of the relaxation techniques in Chapter 10. You can work on these techniques with a team member, like a parent or counselor, until you feel comfortable using them on your own.

You have lots of people in your life who love you and want you to be happy.

No matter what your feelings are or the situation that caused them, there is no reason for you to think that you are alone in dealing with these feelings. It is always good to get feelings out in the open and talk about them with someone. Talking with someone will help you understand what is going on and what you are feeling. You have lots of people in your life who love you and want you to be happy. Your family, your parents, grandparents, a favorite aunt or uncle, or an older brother, sister, or cousin are all there for you. Talking about your emotions is an important step to helping yourself feel better. At school, you can feel safe talking about problems and feelings with your teacher or the counselor. You can also talk to a therapist. Some kids have a very difficult time talking about their feelings, but remember that it gets easier with practice.

To do
list

Reminder

Do not
forget!

Note to self

Remember

Chapter Nine

How Can I Have More Friends?

Maddie had no trouble playing with her old friends, but sometimes she felt out of place or that her friends didn't understand her. When she met new girls, she often became anxious about making a good first impression and wasn't sure what to do. She wished someone would help her and give her some tips on being a better friend and making new ones.

For many girls with AD/HD, friendships come easily and they have lots of friends. They are popular and their friends say they are fun to be around. They never run out of ideas for interesting things to do and usually have a sense of humor and make people laugh. There are also girls with AD/HD who think that they don't have any friends and that no one likes them. Sometimes girls with AD/HD don't know how to make or keep friends. Some girls with AD/HD like Tatiana may prefer to play with boys because they feel more comfortable with them or feel that girls are boring and talk too much. That's okay, too!

Whether you are a girl with lots of friends or one that is having problems making and keeping friends, everyone can improve their friendship skills. In this chapter, let's look at some ways to improve your friendship skills.

Joining a Group

Joining a group of kids that are already friends can be difficult for girls with AD/HD. Do you freeze with anxiety like Samantha when you see others hanging out? Or do you feel that the others are deliberately excluding you like Anna? Do you talk a lot or jump in without waiting to see what is going on? Let's talk about joining in and learn some ways to make this go more smoothly.

There are many ways to successfully join a group of kids that are already friends. Remember, the **STOP! LOOK! LISTEN! and REPEAT!** system we used in Chapter 4? Well, you can use this same system to help make joining a group go more smoothly as well. First, you'll need to **STOP** and take a few minutes to observe the

> **Everyone can improve their friendship skills.**

Christine's Tips on Joining a Group

Here's what I do when I want to join a group:

- Talk about the same topic when there is a stop in the conversation.

- Find the kids on the edges of a group. Sometimes the kids who are not the most popular in the group are the most willing to let you join.

- Look for kids hanging out in smaller groups.

- Rehearse what you want to say to join in.

- Don't interrupt or barge in. Don't be bossy.

Never stay with others who make fun of you or hurt you.

group and see what they are doing. **LOOK** for groups that are friendly and playing safely. Don't try to join groups that clearly don't want you to play or that are playing unsafely or unfairly. Never stay with others who make fun of you or hurt you.

If you then decide that you want to join a group, **STOP** and don't barge in or interrupt the flow of the game that the group is already playing. Wait for a good time to join instead of jumping right in. Next, **LOOK** around and try to find a friendly face in the group. In each group of kids, you will usually find one or two kids who are smiling and who make eye contact with you. Sometimes, these are the kids on the edge of the group or girls that you know or have seen before.

Anna's Tips for Reading Body Language

Here's how I read kids' body language:

- Look for smiling faces.

- Check to see if someone in the group looks at me and acts in a friendly way.

- Notice if someone seems angry (red face, loud voice, raised fists, etc.).

- Check if kids are making fun of or ignoring someone.

- See if girls are whispering in a small group with their heads together shutting out others.

LISTEN to what the kids in the group are saying. Make sure that you know what they are talking about or the rules of the game they are playing before you attempt to join in. Wait for a pause in the conversation or the game and then **REPEAT** a short sentence that conveys your intention to join in. Rehearse what to say ahead of time. "Can I join you?" or "Can I play?" or "Do you want to play?" are all good opening lines.

Remember, don't interrupt or barge in. Don't be bossy or try to take over the group or change the rules. You'll want to make a good first impression on the others in the group, so that they will want to be friends with you.

Making a Good First Impression

How else can you make a good impression? Whether you are making new friends or trying to keep your old ones, there are

Samantha's Tips on Making a Good First Impression

When you want to make a good impression, you should:

- Dress neatly.

- Look the other person in the eye.

- Smile.

- Use the other person's name.

- Wait your turn to speak.

- Say something nice about the other person.

several rules to follow. Here are a few Dos and Don'ts to keep in mind:

Don't brag or talk only about yourself.	Do ask questions about the other person.
Don't do all the talking or interrupt others.	Do give others a chance to talk about themselves.
Don't tease.	Do be friendly.
Don't criticize others.	Do give compliments

Can you think of some other Dos and Don'ts?

Just remember, making and keeping friends is hard work, but with a little practice you'll be an old pro before very long.

> Making and keeping friends is hard work, but with a little practice you'll be an old pro before very long.

Making New Friends

Where else can you look for friends? As a first step, try looking for friends in groups with the same interests that you have, girls who also like ice skating or girls in your scout troop or on your soccer team. Meeting girls that have similar interests or who like doing activities that you are good at will give you a common ground to begin your friendship. That way you may feel less self-conscious or anxious when you're around them.

You might also get to know friends of your relatives (ask your cousins who are about your age to introduce you to their friends), or your friends' friends may be a good place to start. You will have an advantage when playing with these kids since you will have a friend in common right away. You can also look for kids in the neighborhood or at the playground. Sometimes your mom's or dad's friends will have kids your age. Caroline made friends with her mom's running partner's daughter and they played together four days a week while their moms ran. With kids your family hasn't met yet, it also helps to invite your new friends to your home to meet your family. They know a lot about you and can easily tell if a new friend is right for you.

Being a Good Friend

Being a good friend can take work but it's worth it! Friendship comes naturally to some, but not to others. Either way, everyone can learn to be a good (or better) friend. Here are some steps to being a good friend. First, you need to want to be friends with the other person. You may find that you are more comfortable playing with older or younger girls or that you get along better with boys. That's okay! You just need to want to be friends and to feel comfortable with the other person. Second, you need to be loyal to your friends. That means not talking badly about them to others and not excluding them when you're hanging out with someone else. Third, you need to act friendly. That means being generous with your stuff and letting your friend choose the games you play or the movies you watch together. Fourth, you need to be a good listener. Letting your friend talk and not butting in might be hard, but that's how you let your friend know that you care about her and what she thinks.

Remember, any friendship can have difficult moments. Sometimes the best thing that you can do is to say you are sorry or stop doing what hurt the other person. That's not easy for anyone, but it can be the best way to keep a friendship going!

In this chapter, we have talked about ways for you to find more friends or to be a better friend. Of course, not all girls with AD/HD have trouble making and keeping friends, but for some it can be a challenge. If friendships are still difficult for you after you have tried a few of the suggestions in this chapter, don't give up. Learning to be a good friend is just like learning to ride a bike. You have to keep practicing and you'll eventually be good at it!

Chapter Ten

What About My Other Problems?

Now that Maddie had learned how to successfully manage many of the problems related to her AD/HD, she found that she wanted to tackle some of her other problems. Maddie had always had trouble falling asleep at night and at times she would still get an anxious feeling that she had forgotten something important that she had to do for school. Could something be done about these other problems that bothered her?

> **Sometimes just talking about your problems will help you feel better.**

Girls with AD/HD frequently have other problems that bother them. At this point most girls ask, "Now that I know I have AD/HD, what about the other problems AD/HD has caused for me? Is there anything I can do about them?" Having AD/HD may make you feel anxious, sad, or badly about yourself. Because of all the problems you have had to deal with in school, you may not feel so smart. You may get headaches or stomachaches or have problems falling asleep because you are feeling a little stressed out. Let's look at each one of these problems and talk about what you can do to make some of them get better or go away completely.

How Do I Deal With My Anxiety?

Remember Anna? She was anxious and worried a lot. When a girl like Anna has problems paying attention or forgetting things, she can make mistakes or get into trouble. She's often embarrassed by these problems and really doesn't want to get in trouble again. She worries that she has forgotten something or that she will be late or do the wrong thing. Experiencing these situations and feelings over and over again has made her feel sad.

If you find that you are worrying about lots of things like Anna does, it is important to speak with someone about what is bothering you. You can talk with your parents or a counselor at school. Psychologists or therapists, who talk with lots of kids about their feelings and problems, can also help. Sometimes just talking about your problems will help you feel better.

Kids often get headaches and stomachaches when they are stressed or anxious. Dealing well with AD/HD and the problems it causes you will make life easier day to day. It may also help you feel more relaxed and less anxious. When you feel more relaxed and in control, you may find that you have fewer headaches and stomachaches as well. Feeling more relaxed takes practice, so you might have to try some of the tips and techniques on the next page a few times before you feel their full effect. But the practice will be worth it. Here are some techniques you can start using today!

Deep breathing
Progressive muscle relaxation
Yoga
Meditation

Let's take a look at each of these techniques. Maybe you'll find one or two that work for you.

DEEP BREATHING

When something or someone has upset you and you feel anxious or stressed, try deep breathing to help calm yourself. Here's how!

1. Take a deep breath in through your nose while you count to 10.
2. Hold your breath to the count of 4.
3. Let your breath out slowly, blowing through your lips to the count of 10.

Doing this about four or five times should help you feel calmer. This trick is good to remember whenever something upsets you. Breathing slowly and deeply will help drive away those butterflies in your stomach. You can use this kind of breathing anywhere or anytime, when meeting new people or before a test, soccer game, or your piano recital. It will help you calm down and be less anxious.

> Breathing slowly and deeply will help drive away those butterflies in your stomach.

PROGRESSIVE MUSCLE RELAXATION

Progressive muscle relaxation is another great way to help get rid of stress, calm yourself when you are angry, and quiet your mind. If you have trouble settling down during the day or falling asleep at night, try the following exercises to relax your body. By tightening and relaxing the muscles in every part of your body, you can release stress and feel calmer. Try this exercise when you get in bed especially if you have trouble falling asleep at night. Just follow these steps:

1. Start by lying down with your eyes closed.
2. Tighten the muscles in your toes and feet by curling your toes under.
3. Hold this tightening while you count to 10 slowly.
4. Release these muscles and relax, breathing deeply.
5. Tense the muscles in the back of your lower legs by pointing your toes. Hold for a count of 10.
6. Relax.
7. Tighten your upper leg muscles for the count of 10.
8. Relax
9. Tighten the muscles in your stomach. Count to 10.
10. Relax.
11. Keep tightening and holding for the count of 10, all the groups of muscles in your hands, arms, shoulders, neck, and face. (Remember you are only tensing one muscle group at a time.) Then relax and be sure to breathe between each group.
12. When you're finished just lie comfortably with your eyes closed, breathing deeply.

When you finish, you should feel relaxed. Sometimes you might even go to sleep.

Get rid of stress and quiet your mind.

YOGA

Another way to feel relaxed is by practicing yoga. Have you ever done yoga? Yoga combines physical movement, postures, breathing, along with concentration and relaxation to help you feel more in control of your body. Maybe your mom or your older sister knows about yoga. Ask them. You can also take a class, read a book about it, or watch a video to help you learn some of the postures and relaxation techniques.

Clear your mind to feel more in control of your body.

MEDITATION

Meditation is a great tool to help your mind and body feel calm. It combines deep breathing, relaxation, and focusing to clear your mind. Meditation can be difficult to learn even for adults, so don't give up after the first few times that you try. You must practice meditating, but it can be very helpful, particularly if you are feeling very stressed. Meditation can be done walking, sitting, or lying down. Here's how to get started:

1. Sit or lie comfortably in a chair or on the floor with your hands resting in you lap or at your sides. Use a pillow if you need to be more comfortable.
2. Close your eyes and breathe in and out slowly and evenly. Breathe in and count 1. Breathe out and count 2. Continue this slow breathing and counting until you get to 20.
3. After you get to 20, continue breathing in and out very slowly and try to be very still. Think about happy things or let your mind focus on a favorite special place like the beach in summer or a snow covered hill in winter.
4. After a few minutes, take a deep breath in and out to end the meditation.
5. Stretch, stand up, and look all around you, feeling calm and relaxed.

Frannie's Special Meditation Place

When I'm trying to relax, I meditate and focus on my favorite place, the beach. I think about:

- The ocean's many shades of blue.

- The noise of the waves as they crash on the shore.

- The scent of the salty ocean air.

- The cries of seagulls and other birds.

- The warm breeze on my face and bare arms and legs.

- The hot sand under my feet.

- The sun shining down, warming my skin.

- The large boats far off in the water.

GETTING OUTSIDE

Another good way to relax and feel less stressed is to get outdoors. Getting a lot of fresh air and exercise will help you feel better and may even help you sleep better at night. Experts have even found that kids with AD/HD who spend more time in green spaces (outside your house or in a park) are less hyperactive. That's really a good thing. There are so many things you can do alone or with friends and family. You could:

Walk your dog
Garden
Fly a kite

Turn off the TV and GET GOING!

Climb trees with friends

Play freeze tag

So what are you waiting for? Turn off the TV and GET GOING!

What About My Sleep Problems?

Sleep is important for everyone in order to be healthy and to have good memory and concentration. If you don't get a good night's sleep, your brain and body will be tired the next day. You'll be less alert, more irritable, and definitely not at your best. Getting a full night's sleep is even more important if you have AD/HD.

There are many reasons for not being able to fall asleep at night. Sometimes you might not want to stop what you are doing and go to bed. But for some kids with AD/HD like Maddie, falling asleep can be a really big problem. If you have trouble falling asleep, you might want to ask yourself: Did I not get enough exercise during the day? Am I hungry? Am I overtired from staying up too late because I didn't get my homework done earlier? Have I just watched a TV show or movie or played a video game that has left me overstimulated?

If you answered "yes" to any of these questions, these are easy fixes. Simple things like getting more exercise, making sure you've eaten well, getting to bed on-time, or watching more relaxing shows may make a big difference. Make whatever change to correct that specific situation and see if that helps you sleep any better.

But sometimes, kids with AD/HD have trouble settling down and falling asleep because they are worried or anxious like Anna. Having lots of worries and other thoughts swirling around in your head may prevent you from sleeping. If this happens to you, be

Having lots of worries may prevent you from sleeping.

sure to tell someone. You and your parents can then work to help you settle down at night. You can also work together to come up with a set bedtime or a night routine. Let's try to think of some other ways to make bedtime calmer so you can get to sleep easier. Here are a few ideas that might work for you:

- Take a nice long relaxing bath.
- Have a glass of warm milk or a small snack. Make sure that the snack doesn't have a lot of sugar or caffeine that might keep you awake.
- Listen to quiet music.
- Avoid watching TV, playing video games, or reading an exciting book right before bedtime. That might keep you awake.

Attention, Attention!

Some healthy bedtime snacks are:

- Whole wheat bagel with lowfat cream cheese

- Celery or crackers with peanut butter

- A small bowl of soup

- Frozen whole wheat waffles

- Yogurt with fruit

- Bowl of nutritious cereal

Avoid cereals or other snacks with lots of sugar, additives and food colorings like cookies, pastries, doodles, and colored drinks and sodas.

- Try to have your bedroom as dark as you can. Make sure you have blinds or shades on the windows and that the door is closed. If you need a nightlight, try to have it on in the hallway or behind the bed where it doesn't shine in your eyes.
- Pack your backpack and go over tomorrow's schedule with your parents before getting in bed. That way you won't stay awake worrying that you have forgotten something important.
- Think about something pleasant and relaxing. Having your favorite stuffed animal, a picture you like, or a keepsake from a fun vacation (like a shell from the beach) near you to look at may help you relax and calm down.
- Try progressive muscle relaxation (look on page 103). This tool has been found to help people relax and get to sleep.

After trying a few of these ideas, if you are still having problems falling asleep, it is probably time for you to discuss this problem with your parents and doctor.

What About My Sensitivities?

Instead of feeling grumpy, talk about what's bothering you.

Do you remember the girl named Georgia who we met in Chapter 2? She was grumpy and irritable all the time because lots of things bothered her? Tags in her clothes. Loud noises. Getting her hair washed or her face wet. Some foods also felt funny on her tongue and she didn't like to eat them. Because so many things bother her, Georgia is often cranky. When she cries and refuses to eat or to do something, her mom often doesn't know why and gets angry with her.

If you have any of the problems Georgia has, instead of feeling grumpy and then crying or yelling, talk about what is bothering you with your mom and dad. Once they understand how you feel, they can help. Tell them what clothes feel good on your body and what foods you like and don't like. You can also discuss ways to make your shower or bath more enjoyable. Washing, drying, and brushing your hair yourself, will help you to feel more comfortable and in control. Once in a while, don't forget to take a chance and do something you haven't tried before. Then reward yourself just for trying. As you get older, your sensitivities will lessen, but you might be surprised at what you can do now.

If noises bother you, there are lots of things you can try to make that better as well. Wear headphones or earplugs to block out noises when you are trying to concentrate or do homework. Try to be prepared for loud noises. If you know ahead of time when a loud noise like the school bell or a horn is coming, you won't be as surprised and scared by it. You can also cover your ears in preparation. If a loud noise

Attention, Attention!

Taste and texture sensitivities can be annoying. Here are some tips to deal with them:

- **Food**: Choose bland foods that you will eat. Foods like macaroni and cheese, applesauce, bagels, soup, and plain cereals are good.

- **Touch**: Have your parent cut out tags in clothing and buy socks without seams. Clothes should be soft and not tight. Elastic waistbands are usually best.

- **Bathing and Hair Washing**: Try pouring the water on your own head. Also, use a detangler spray before brushing your hair. Some girls also like a shower better than a bath.

happens and you do get bothered, try the relaxation techniques we talked about, like taking deep breaths to calm yourself down.

Remember, you don't need to work on all of these things that bother you by yourself. There are experts in helping kids just like you deal with these same problems. They are called occupational therapists. Occupational therapists work with your body and give you exercises to help decrease your sensitivities. If you continue to have difficulty, even after you try some of these tips or if your sensitivities are causing you problems so that you avoid activities or feel irritable all the time, get help. Your teacher, your counselor, or your doctor should know the name of an occupational therapist in your area that can help you and your parents with a program to make things better. There are also lots of books to learn more about these problems.

Whether it's learning to relax, getting to sleep at night, or dealing with your sensitivities, I hope that you have found some helpful suggestions in this chapter. And I hope that you have learned that no matter what the problem is, there is always something that you can do about it! Taking action to solve a problem lets you feel in control. Remember, you never need to face problems alone. Your support team is there to help you!

Part Four

Do Your Research!

Build on
What You've Learned!

Well, you've finished *Attention, Girls!* and I hope you've learned a lot about AD/HD and even more about yourself. You now have many new tips and strategies to manage your AD/HD and the ways it can affect your life. But reading this book is just the beginning. There are still so many things for you to learn! In the next section, I've put together a list of books to help you learn more about AD/HD and to help you get control over many of the problems that it may cause for you. I have also listed some books that contain stories about kids like you. (It's always fun to read about others.) This list is not exhaustive, so visit your local library, ask your teachers and school counselor, talk to your friends, and do some research online to find additional books and resources on AD/HD. Who knows? It could be fun!

In *Attention, Girls!* we have talked about lots of people (like doctors, therapists, tutors, and coaches) who are available to help you feel and do better. At school, you have teachers, principals, counselors, and psychologists, who you can talk with when you are having problems or just feel overwhelmed. Your parents and family understand and love you and they will make sure that you get all the help you need. Remember for them to be able to help you, you have to do your part. Be honest with yourself and tell people when things are difficult or when you feel discouraged or sad. People can't help if they don't know something is wrong or bothering you! One way to do this is to write about your AD/HD. Writing about yourself and your AD/HD is a great way to share your story and your feelings with your family and friends. You will need to work hard with your teachers, therapists, tutors, and family. But in the end it will all be worth it!

As you grow older, your AD/HD may affect you in different ways. You might develop problems (either physically or socially) that you don't have right now or some of your problems might lessen or go away altogether. That's why it's important that you keep learning about yourself and about AD/HD. But remember . . . AD/HD isn't who you are. It is just one part of what makes up that wonderful, unique person—YOU!

Wishing you much happiness and success!

Patricia O. Quinn, MD

$\mathcal{M}$ore Resources for You!

Books for Kids

TO LEARN MORE ABOUT AD/HD

Putting on the Brakes, Second Edition: Understanding and Taking Control of Your ADD or ADHD by Patricia O. Quinn, MD and Judith M. Stern, MA (Magination Press)

Learning to Slow Down and Pay Attention: A Book for Kids About ADHD, Third Edition by Kathleen Nadeau, PhD and Ellen Dixon (Magination Press)

The Survival Guide for Kids with ADD and ADHD by John Taylor (Free Spirit Publishing)

TO READ ABOUT KIDS WITH AD/HD

Sparky's Excellent Misadventures: My ADD Journal, By Me (Sparky) by Phyllis Carpenter and Marti Ford (Magination Press)

Cory Stories: A Kid's Book About Living with ADHD by Jeanne Kraus (Magination Press)

The Adventures of Phoebe
Flower by Barbara Roberts
(Advantage Books)

   That's What Kids Are For
   Phoebe's Lost Treasure
   Phoebe's Best Best Friend
   Phoebe's Tree House
     Secrets

Joey Pigza Swallowed
a Key by Jack Gantos
(Harper Collins
Children's Books)

Eagle Eyes: A Child's
Guide to Paying Attention by
Jeanne Gehret (Verbal Images
Press)

Jumpin' Johnny Get Back to Work by
Michael Gordon (GSI Publications)

Ethan Has Too Much Energy by Lawrence Shapiro (Boulden
Publishing)

TO LEARN ABOUT MEDICATION FOR AD/HD

Otto Learns About His Medicine: A Story About Medication for
Children With ADHD, Third Edition by Matthew Galvin, MD
(Magination Press)

TO HAVE FUN LEANING ABOUT AD/HD

Putting on the Brakes Activity Book for Kids with ADD or ADHD, Second Edition by Patricia O. Quinn, MD and Judith M. Stern, MA (Magination Press)

50 Games and Activities for Kids with ADHD by Patricia O. Quinn, MD and Judith M. Stern, MA (Magination Press)

TO HELP YOU DO BETTER IN SCHOOL

Annie's Plan: Taking Charge of Schoolwork and Homework by Jeanne Kraus (Magination Press)

Many Ways to Learn: Young People's Guide to Learning Disabilities by Judith Stern, MA and Uzi Ben-Ami, PhD (Magination Press)

The School Survival Guide for Kids with Learning Differences by Rhonda Cummings and Gary Fisher (Free Spirit Publishing)

Get Organized without Losing It by Janet Fox and Pamela Espeland (Free Spirit Publishing)

True or False? Tests Stink! by Trevor Romain and Elizabeth Verdick (Free Spirit Publishing)

How to Do Homework without Throwing Up by Trevor Romain (Free Spirit Publishing)

How to Be School Smart: Super Study Skills by Elizabeth James and Carol Barkin (Beech Tree Books)

TO HELP WITH FEELINGS AND BEHAVIORS

What-to-Do Guides for Kids by Dawn Huebner, PhD (Magination Press)

  What to Do When You Worry Too Much: A Kid's Guide to Overcoming Anxiety
  What to Do When You Grumble Too Much: A Kid's Guide to Overcoming Negativity

What to Do When Your Temper Flares: A Kid's Guide to Overcoming Problems with Anger

What to Do When You Dread Your Bed: A Kid's Guide to Overcoming Problems with Sleep

What to Do When Bad Habits Take Hold: A Kid's Guide to Overcoming Nail Biting and More

Mind Over Basketball: Coach Yourself to Handle Stress by Jane Weierbach, PhD and Elizabeth Phillips-Hershey, PhD (Magination Press)

Nobody's Perfect: A Story for Children About Perfectionism by Ellen Flanagan Burns (Magination Press)

The Behavior Survival Guide for Kids: How to Make Good Choices and Stay Out of Trouble by Thomas McIntyre (Free Spirit Publishing)

Doing and Being Your Best by Pamela Espeland and Elizabeth Verdick (Free Spirit Publishing)

See You Later, Procrastinator! (Get It Done) by Pamela Espeland and Elizabeth Verdick (Free Spirit Publishing)

Stress Can Really Get on Your Nerves by Trevor Romain and Elizabeth Verdick (Free Spirit Publishing)

The Feelings Book: The Care & Keeping of Your Emotions by Lynda Madison, PhD (American Girl)

TO HELP YOU MAKE AND KEEP FRIENDS

Circle of Three: Enough Friendship to Go Around? by Elizabeth Brokamp (Magination Press)

Too Nice by Marjorie White Pellegrino (Magination Press)

Cliques, Phonies, & Other Baloney by Trevor Romain (Free Spirit Publishing)

A Smart Girls Guide to Friendship Troubles: Dealing with Fights, Being Left Out, & the Whole Popularity Thing by Patti Kelley Criswell (American Girl)

TO HELP YOU UNDERSTAND SENSORY PROBLEMS

Meghan's World: The Story of One Girl's Triumph Over Sensory Processing Disorder by Diane M. Renna (Indigo Impressions)

The Goodenoughs Get in Sync by Carol Stock Kranowitz (Sensory Resources)

Books for Parents

TO LEARN MORE ABOUT AD/HD

Parenting Children with ADHD: 10 Lessons That Medicine Cannot Teach by Vincent J. Monastra, PhD (APA Books)

Taking Charge of ADHD: The Complete, Authoritative Guide for Parents (Revised Edition) by Russell A. Barkley, PhD (Guilford Press)

ADHD: Survival Guide for Parents and Teachers by Richard A. Lougy, MFT and David K. Rosenthal, MD (Hope Press)

TO LEARN ABOUT MEDICATIONS FOR AD/HD

Straight Talk about Psychiatric Medications for Kids, Third Edition by Timothy E. Wilens, MD (Guilford Press)

TO HELP YOUR KIDS MAKE FRIENDS

Why Don't They Like Me? Helping Your Child Make and Keep Friends by Susan M. Sheridan (Sopris West)

How to Raise Your Child's Social IQ by Cathi Cohen (Advantage Books)

Nobody Likes Me, Everybody Hates Me: The Top 25 Friendship Problems and How to Solve Them by Michele Borba, EdD (Jossey-Bass)

TO UNDERSTAND SENSORY PROBLEMS

The Out-of-Sync Child: Recognizing and Coping with Sensory Processing Disorder, Revised Edition by Carol Stock Kranowitz (Perigee Trade)

The Out-of-Sync Child Has Fun by Carol Stock Kranowitz and T.J. Wylie (Perigee Trade)

The Everything Parent's Guide to Sensory Integration Disorder: Get the Right Diagnosis, Understand Treatments, and Advocate for Your Child by Terri Mauro (Adams Media)

Parenting a Child with Sensory Processing Disorder: A Family Guide to Understanding & Supporting Your Sensory-Sensitive Child by Christopher R. Auer, MA and Susan L. Blumberg, PhD (New Harbinger)

The Highly Sensitive Child: Helping Our Children Thrive When the World Overwhelms Them by Elaine N. Aron, PhD (Broadway Books)

Do not forget!